Man Up!

BECOMING THE NEW
CATHOLIC RENAISSANCE MAN

JARED ZIMMERER

Foreword by Fr. Dwight Longenecker

Contributors include:
Jim Burnham
Marlon DeLaTorre
Deacon Harold Burke-Sivers
Fr. Steve Grunow
Jesse Romero
Kevin Vost
Shane Kapler
Douglas Bushman
Kevin Lowry
Gerard-Marie Anthony
Dave Dinuzzo

© 2014 by Jared Zimmerer

Published by
Bezalel Books
Waterford, MI
www.BezalelBooks.com

The choicest first fruits of your soil you shall bring to the house of the Lord, your God. ~Exodus 23:19

We would like to thank all Catholic priests. Through your courage and witness you lead all men to authentic masculinity

Printed in the United States of America

Cover Art: © Claudio Balducelli | Dreamstime.com

ISBN 978-1-936453-16-0
Library of Congress Control Number 2013906438

The Benedictine Gentleman

FOREWORD BY
FR. DWIGHT LONGENECKER

Think what it would be like if the US Government went bust. I mean really went bust and there was no way anybody was going to lend the United States any more money. Let's imagine that there is no money to pay the police or the National Guard. No money to pay school teachers or fund the state universities. The government offices close down. The border patrol men lay down their equipment. The technology infrastructure collapses. The financial system implodes. Everything goes down like a house of cards.

The hungry unemployed start prowling around like packs of wolves. Then imagine that the lawless drug lords of Mexico and the hungry hoards South of the Border start to sweep into the United States raping, plundering and pillaging as they go.

That was the world of St Benedict. By the end of the fifth century the Roman Empire was crumbling. The great Roman armies went without pay, deserted and drifted home. The barbarians swept in from the North and the East. The great city of Rome was sacked and everything came crashing down.

In the midst of this chaos St Benedict was a survivalist. He went to the hills south of Rome with a handful of men and established small self sufficient communities. Those communities were the strongholds not only of survival but civilization, and the civilization that those first monks preserved eventually blossomed into the great culture we call Christendom.

St Benedict the Gentleman

St Benedict hunkered down with his fellow monks to establish an ordered life in the midst of chaos. He came from a noble family and he brought a tradition of nobility, courtesy and dignity to the heart of his communities. The communities he founded became the seed bed for the establishment of a whole new Christian society, and that society was founded on the ideal of what I call the Christian gentleman.

By "gentleman" I do not mean an effete dandy with a purple vest, pointed shoes, a boutonniere and Brylcreamed hair. Neither do I mean an English sort of gentleman with a clipped mustache, a clipped accent and clipped masculinity. By "gentleman" I mean a nobleman, or a man that is noble. By "noble" I don't mean that he is from an aristocratic caste or castle, but that he is a man of classic virtue, learning, honesty and courage. He knows what is right and will stand for what is beautiful, good and true courage and without compromise. He is a truly noble knight.

St Benedict called his monasteries "schools for the Lord's service." He used military language, saying that the monks were "soldiers of Christ" and his strict discipline was a means to an end, and the end was to establish an atmosphere in which strong soldiers could be trained for the spiritual warfare of the age.

Such noble knights of the spirit were needed to counter the disintegration of the culture, the threat of the heathen hoards and the violence of the barbarians. When I talk about Benedict and his age to men's groups they invariably agree with me that our own society is at the point where such survivalist communities may become necessary.

Benedict the Balanced

What is remarkable about St Benedict is that, in a brutal and chaotic age, he does not resort to violence and defense, but builds communities of gentle prayer, refined order and the love of God and neighbor. The life of the Benedictine gentleman is built on two sets of three principles. The monk's vows and the three fold way of life.

For those who wish to follow Christ in the way of St Benedict, there are many books written to expound the way. Put simply and briefly, the Benedictine monk makes vows of obedience, stability and conversion of life. These three vows complement each other and provide the foundation for a solid and balanced life.

The vow of obedience teaches all of us that we are subject to something and someone greater than ourselves. The fact of the matter is, the majority of things in our lives we have no control over. We are therefore obedient to those factors in life to which we must submit. Every Christian man must establish to whom he answers. If we are to be soldiers of Christ we should know who our commanding officer is. The Catholic Church provides just such a framework, and the weak kneed individualism of our age is countered by a manly response of obedience. For the monk the vow of stability means remaining a loyal member of one particular community for life. He stays put. He does not go searching for a better life somewhere else. He learns that God is not elsewhere. For Catholic men the vow of stability teaches us that we need to settle down and be mature. Our wives and children need us to be rock solid, dependable and reliable. They want adventure, but they also want stability and security. We're the source of the stability they need to grow strong.

The vow of conversion of life means that every effort of the monk is directed toward the final and complete transformation of his life into the image of Christ. The Catholic man also learns from this vow and sets his priorities. Everything is ordered to the love of Christ. Every habit, every temptation, every desire, every ambition, every penny, every possession is directed toward the purification of the soul, the salvation of the world and the love of Christ. No compromise.

The Threefold Way

These three vows are put into practice by the threefold life of the monastery. This means that everything the monk does falls into one of three categories: Work, Prayer and Reading (or study). The three are like three strands in a braided rope. They are intertwined and support one another.

In the modern world these three categories can still encompass all our activities. Work ennobles man. Work is good and not only earns our bread, but gives our lives meaning and structure. The New Testament teaches, "If a man does not work, neither should he eat." Honest work drives away the devil and accomplishes God's creativity in the world.

Prayer is the cornerstone of the Benedictine life and the practical approach to prayer taught by Benedict is relevant and rich for the modern Catholic man. The Benedictine principle of prayer is that it is short and frequent. In the modern world we can weave short effective prayers into our work day so the prayer sanctifies the work and the work grounds the prayer.

The third aspect of the Benedictine life is study. For the modern man I suggest that 'study' or reading includes all forms of stimulus from sources outside ourselves. Leisure activities like sports and the arts can be a form of 'reading'. A decent movie or television series can be as stimulating as a book. However, nothing can replace the depth of experience and learning as old fashioned "curling up with a good book."

Through these three aspects of life the Christian gentleman develops his body, mind and spirit and establishes the wise balance made famous by Benedict and his monks.

Benedict and this Book

Jared Zimmerer has brought together all these themes by collecting a gang of experts in authentic Catholic masculinity. Jesse Romero wades in with fighting talk about the need to be warriors of Christ and Jared's essay echoes the theme by telling how to be a Catholic warrior today. Meanwhile Marlon de la Torre and Deacon Burke-Sivers dig deep in the development of the intellect. Kevin Vost gives pointers on the importance of study while Father Grunow deepens the life of prayer through the sacraments.

This book weaves in practical pointers on the conversion of life through Douglas Bushman and Jim Burnham teaching on authentic masculine sexuality, our role as providers, husbands and fathers and Kevin Lowry helps us manage our work -life balance with true nobility and generosity of spirit. Dave Dinuzzo winds up with an essay on how to overcome pornography and concludes with a rousing call to arms.

Some feel that our own society—like ancient Rome—teeters on the brink of chaos and collapse. St Benedict's authentic Christian communities were the seeds that flowered into the greatest civilization history has seen—Christian Europe. The foundations laid by Benedict's communities of Catholic gentlemen supported an edifice that was beautiful, strong and true. From those communities flowered learning, science, literature, music, the university system, the judicial system and philosophies which still nurture our culture today.

Let us hope and pray that this book will play its part in inspiring a twenty first century army of Catholic gentleman...renaissance noble men who will lead a new resurrection.

Fr Dwight Longenecker is the pastor of Our Lady of the Rosary Church in Greenville, South Carolina. He is a Benedictine oblate of Belmont Abbey and the author of Listen My Son, St Benedict for Fathers. Visit his blog, browse his books and be in touch at dwightlongenecker.com

Where Have All The Good Men Gone?

JARED ZIMMERER

In recent history manliness, or the idea of authentic masculinity, has experienced a jolt of interest. The liberalistic, progressive culture of the United States today has created disarray within the minds of boys falling into a manhood characterized by deviancy and immoral revelry. Men today seem confused about what it means to be a man. While in the past, from the Greek philosophers to the early 1900's, men would joke about and investigate what it meant to be a man in order to discover that truth, making it a topic of discussion, today this subject is jeered at, passed over and thought unnecessary. However, the successes of books like *Be A Man!* by Fr. Larry Richards and *The Art of Manliness* by Brett McKay tells of the innate desire of all men to know what our role is in this world.

While the liberal culture offers television shows like *The Man Show* or *Two and a Half Men* filled with men acting like children, Catholic culture offers saints of benevolent virtue and honor, who have embarked upon adventurous deeds of bravery, courage, and unswerving loyalty to their faith. Nevertheless, most of today's men desire to be like the men seen in movies such as *The Hangover,* or in shows akin to *Jersey Shore,* both of which portray men as daft sexual prowlers. History, however, proves that the hearts of males are drawn towards the ideals of integrity and resolve, as shown by the success of movies like *Braveheart* and *Gladiator.* Men feel in their souls that they want to be the next William Wallace or Socrates, but the society that has raised them has created a being more akin to Baby Huey or Machiavelli's Prince—men completely out for themselves yet unable to control their base instincts for comfort and entitlement.

In order to truly appreciate the following chapters showing why and how Catholicism creates the definitive male, one needs to understand why it is necessary to outline masculinity. The term *liberal culture* has many connotations meaning different things to different people. Discerning different definitions of liberalism goes all the way back to the early 16th century, when liberal philosophy was defined as "freedom from restraint"—meaning free thought and the ability to decide what is best for oneself. I do not intend to give credence to the liberal movement as it has had its own confrontations with our holy Catholic Church; this is however the philosophy of our culture and the culture in which men are raised today. While a few of the ideas presented in the liberal culture—independence and fairness, for example—do agree with Catholic values, issues have arisen since the beginning of the laissez-faire mentality. What I intend to show is that what was once a school of moral and ethical thought has now become a basis for licentiousness and decadence, which ultimately leads to a decline in honest, hardworking, chaste men.

Liberalism has become something completely foreign to its original meaning; today it is a word interchangeable with *relativism*. What once was a notion of free thought and openness to new ideas—both very Catholic virtues, by the way—has now become the belief that every type of religion, philosophy, or behavior is acceptable, even if they create evil because, as is consistent with progressive, modernist ideologies, even evil is in the eye of the beholder. It is portrayed as a matter of personal interpretation. Nowadays, liberalism has become the acceptance of anything and anyone. Be they immoral, immodest or confused the culture now says that we should not judge people by their actions or character; we should judge them by how well they adhere to their own personal truths.

The original theories proposed by Thomas Hobbes and John Locke held mankind in such a high regard that they believed men could rule themselves, free of any form of government, because men were infused with a natural law. The founders of this movement believed that man had a conscience and had the willpower to follow it, a belief stemming from their intellectual respect for an all-encompassing truth. Today, however, the idea of conscience, in this sense, is lost on the modern liberal. Modernists now see conscience as a psychological ball and chain, dragging one down into the pit of despair. But, rather, as Thomas Jefferson queried: "Can the liberties of a nation be thought secure when we have removed their only firm basis, a conviction in the minds of the people that these liberties are of the gift of God?" (*Notes on the State of Virginia*, Ch. 18) Eventually, a secular, liberal culture will lead to an atheistic society because if there is not a higher, God-given truth to which all other purported truths must correspond, then ultimately no truth is worth following. In other words, liberalistic relativism has been tried and left wanting in the hearts of honest, God-fearing men.

Relating progressive liberalism to our subject of authentic masculinity, the question must be asked: Can a man of worth and honor live by the ideals of "I'm OK, You're OK"?

In order to answer this question, one must examine the philosophy at issue and how it relates to manhood. If a real man loves truth, even when truth blatantly disagrees with his personal belief system, then relativism is unmanly. If a real man desires what is best for his family and works hard to create opportunities for his children to succeed, he cannot agree with the liberals who tell parents not to make choices for their children and instead to make sure that their children go in the direction that passions and pressures lead them. If a real man is one that desires to form his children's conscience in truth, he would not allow them to believe in anything that is not absolutely right in the eyes of God.

The current state of progressive liberalism does not allow for any philosophies that portray black-and-white statements of immutable truth. Put another way, it believes that what might be your idea of truth may not be theirs. As Pontius Pilate famously scoffed, "What is Truth?" (John 18:30) On the contrary, true masculinity cannot reside in the gray area; either an action is wrong or it is right. In his *Apology,* Plato impeccably argues that "a man who is good for anything ought not to calculate the chance of living or dying; he ought only to consider whether in doing anything he is doing right or wrong—acting the part of a good man or bad."

In a culture as liberal as ours, one is forbidden to choose a value or faith worth dying for because that elevates one's truth above someone else's, which, according to modernists, is just plain bad manners. It is interesting to note that in a world as lost as ours, people of virtue and kindness are perceived as weak; and yet it was immoral behavior that brought Rome to its knees. It can cripple our country as well if things are not turned around.

The progressive liberal culture breeds moral inadequacy within males, creating men of childish, selfish, and barbaric behavior. Three models of masculinity have evolved from our current society. First is the "hooligan" who has no respect for anything or anyone and who seeks to engender fear in the hearts of those who come into contact with him. An example of this type might be a member of the many street gangs found throughout the United States.

The second model is the "man-boy" who lacks motivation and worships the ideals of Peter Pan, crying out "I don't want to grow up." His selfish behavior resembles that of Hugh Hefner, using women as a kind of plaything and living for the next party. One doesn't need to search very far for this type of false manhood; most college campuses, dive bars and clubs are full of them.

The third model is the person endowed with physical male attributes, yet resonates none of them; his attitude and clothing bespeak femininity, but he claims to be a boy. The term "metrosexual", which was coined in 1994, refers to a man who is so narcissistically involved with himself that he spends all of his time, money, and energy making himself up to resemble a fashion model such as might be seen in *GQ*. In an article called "Meet the Metrosexual" published by *Salon.com,* Mark Simpson, the man most usually credited with coining the term, describes this archetype by saying "he might be officially gay, straight or bisexual, but this is utterly immaterial because he has clearly taken himself as his own love object and pleasure as his sexual preference."

A true, God-fearing, Catholic man does not fall into any of these classifications. In fact, Catholic manhood is in such staunch opposition to these three models that the current secular culture revels in derisive laughter at it and suffers from misunderstanding to the point of discrimination against such men. St. Augustine dealt with very similar problems, as indicated in one of his sermons: "Man's wickedness is now such that men are more ashamed of chastity than of lechery..... If any man has the nerve to say that he is chaste and faithful to his wife and this gets known, he is ashamed to mix with other men, whose behavior is not like his, for they will mock him and despise him and say he's not a real man; for man's wickedness is now of such proportions that no one is considered a man unless he is overcome by lechery, while one who overcomes lechery and stays chaste is considered unmanly." (*Sermons* #1-19)

Many of the men I have described have grown up in fatherless homes, attesting to the fact that the male role models they choose to identify with are those of the secular culture. If the father is absent, a male child will find someone else to imitate. According to the U.S. Census Bureau 24 million children in America—one out of three—live in homes without a biological father. (Current Population Reports, p. 70-104. Table 1. Washington, DC: U.S. Census Bureau, 2005.) The same bureau also concludes that 63% of youth suicides are from fatherless homes, as are 70% of juveniles in state-operated institutions. Similarly, "man-boys" and metrosexual fops often come from a fatherless home as well. "Boys who grow up in father-absent homes are more likely than those in father-present homes to have trouble establishing appropriate sex roles and gender identity." (P.L. Adams, J.R. Milner, and N.A. Schrepf, *Fatherless Children*, New York, Wiley Press, 1984). The relativistic Playboy culture has given credence to the idea of men wanting to live for their own pleasure and satisfaction, of men abandoning their wives and children, having decided that it is against their own personal "truth" to stay and be a good role model. The connection between fatherless homes and distorted models of masculine identity demonstrates that the dominating liberal ideals cannot and will not create better men.

Aside from the liberal philosophies of today already discussed, there are a few other ideological influences that have attempted (and might I say have succeeded in some areas) to emasculate men—and to masculinize women. While a real man never blames others for his own problems, nevertheless it must be recognized that radical leftist feminism has created a thoroughly ominous presence surrounding the growth of boys into men. While many feminists simply want their fair share—which is admirable enough in its own right—there are some out there who would prefer to do away with men in general. Andrea Dworkin, a famous staunch feminist, wrote "I want to see a man beaten to a bloody pulp with a high-heel shoved in his mouth, like an apple in the mouth of a pig." (*Ice and Fire*, Weidenfeld & Nicholson, 1987) The radical feminists of today have contributed to the phenomenon of men fearing their own manliness. Imposing visions of murderous barbarians on those men whose only desire is to fulfill their role as leaders has caused men to cower in times of conflict. Lies like "...sex and murder are fused in the male consciousness, so that the one without the imminent possibility of the other is unthinkable and impossible" (Andrea Dworkin, *Letters from a War Zone*, Dutton

Publishing, 1989) are consistently voiced on college campuses and among the intellectual elite.

One of the many tactics of radical feminism over the last century has been to spread a lie and repeat it over and over until it becomes a truth. "Men are pigs" has become a repeated, rhetorical statement that has been used so much that even men believe it now. The anger of radical feminists toward the ideals of man as head of the household or man as the leader of society has permeated our culture. The stereotype of men as idiotic children who can at most open a beer and watch football is an underlying proposition of the feminist movement. It is the foundational reason why we see so frequently on television the oft-repeated theme of young women making a name for themselves and the men trying to latch on and reap the benefits. Boys are no longer raised to become leaders or innovators.

The radical feminist movement has also caused great confusion in the area of marriage and gender roles. "Since marriage constitutes slavery for women, it is clear that... freedom for women cannot be won without the abolition of marriage," says Sheila Cronan, the leader of the feminist organization NOW. (*Radical Feminism "Marriage"*, HarperCollins, 1973, p. 219) Even the idea of an equal partnership between a man and a woman isn't thought ideal; for the progressive feminist it must be the woman in charge, or she is being oppressed. "Being a housewife is an illegitimate profession... The choice to serve and be protected and plan towards being a family-maker is a choice that shouldn't be. The heart of radical feminism is to change that." (Vivian Gornick, feminist author, University of Illinois, *The Daily Illini*, April 25, 1981.)

Feminism has unfortunately lost its original ideals of equal rights and opportunities, both very admirable goals. While women deserve our utmost respect and love, radical feminists have "changed the ballgame" so to speak. Radical women activists have created a time in which men feel awkward pulling out the chair for them to sit or to hold open the door for them to walk through. Successful women in the limelight now no longer feel they need a man to raise a family. I think William Bray said it best in his work, *The Emasculation of American Men: 50 Reasons Why Males are No Longer Men:* "We are witnessing a society in which women have gained independence and equality with the male on many fronts and accomplishments. However, in the process, in the wake, of those accomplishments males are being put down and women stepping up, on and over them to reach their goals. In this male battering process males have been psychologically emasculated…good house servants for the newly emancipated females."

Feminism, liberalism, and many other "isms" have quietly and confidently stripped away the ideals of the past, especially when it comes to the role of men in society, politics, and most importantly, familial relationships. A devout faith and solid loyalty to the truths of the Catholic Church are the means to bring light into the darkness of masculinity confusion. The misperception of a masculine faith-life along with the emasculation of church services and ministries has lured the latest generations of males away from church altogether, which studies show causes a decrease in overall church attendance. If we want to turn the ship of faithlessness around in this country and the world, we must begin with the men reassuming their roles as the spiritual heads of their households. In an article entitled *The Truth About Men & Church: On the Importance of Fathers to Churchgoing*, Robbie Low states that "if the father is non-practicing and [the] mother regular, only 2 percent of children will become regular worshippers, and 37 percent will attend irregularly. Over 60 percent of their children will be lost completely to the church. What happens if the father is regular but the mother irregular or non-practicing? Extraordinarily, the percentage of children becoming regular goes up … to 38 percent." A man's role is undeniable when it comes to raising his children as devout, God-fearing citizens.

The faith of males today has dwindled down to the idea of wearing a rosary around one's neck and claiming to be Christian, although the lifestyle of these so-called Christians would definitely say otherwise. Seen as a good luck charm, faith is now viewed as something only the weak need, yet even the "manliest" of men who have no fear of life or death tend to become spineless little cowards when asked to step into a church. I have seen numerous men claiming the title of grandiosity in worldly terms who tuck their tail and run when it's time to pray or go to Mass. Men "too cool" to lead a prayer service or to sing during the liturgy are numerous and raising yet another generation who believe faith is nothing more than superstition and is unmanly. The same men willing to work 80 hours a week in order to afford a new toy of some kind are somehow too busy to take their families to Mass on Sundays.

Faith in God and an active spiritual life, vivified through daily devotion to prayer and the practice of regular confession and reception of Holy Communion are undeniably important facets of the Catholic man. Self-discipline and manhood stem from the acceptance of a man's role as a created being, owing his allegiance to unending, infallible truth. Freedom of conscience and will reside within the Word of God, "If you remain in my word, you will truly be my disciples, and you will know the truth, and the truth will set you free" (Jn 8:31-32). As Jesus is the Way, the Truth and the Life, each and every human being is indebted to Christ for the salvation of their souls. Men's hearts, knowing and loving the sacrificial nature of martyrdom, can see the legitimate use of giving up one's life for freedom. Religion—and most especially the Catholic Faith—offers opportunities for daily sacrifices: physical, mental or spiritual. That is manly.

Our culture is one of extremes. In the case of boys growing up today their role models consist of the chauvinistic pigs that feminists rant about, the "Peter Pans" living in eternal boyhood, or the metrosexual dandies who have lost their grit and are in want of a backbone. Real, honest-to-goodness men of moral and spiritual strength are far and few between. As the self-apparent decline of all things moral has taken place, the men are the beings designed by God to take a stand and say, *enough!* The world needs superheroes to emulate and to depend upon. The new Catholic Renaissance man—of whom you will learn about throughout this book—can be that hero. Stout in mind, prepared in body and magnanimous in soul, sternly devoted to the masculine aspects of his Catholic Faith, the new Catholic man will always rise to the occasion of holiness and true freedom.

Do Not Be Afraid of the Culture of Death

JESSE ROMERO

I am a retired Deputy Sheriff, a black belt in Karate, a former kick-boxing and boxing champion. My three kids are all very athletic; my two boys are accomplished and ferocious wrestlers. I am also an expert with nunchucks (Chinese fighting sticks attached with a chain) and was an expert in firearms with the Los Angeles Sheriff's Department. Today, I still train my boys and other teenagers in Mixed Martial Arts. My background is one of self-defense and competitive fighting.

When I truly converted to the Catholic faith with my whole heart and made Jesus the Lord of my life (back in 1988), I brought into this new way of Christian living all of my competitive fighting background. St Thomas Aquinas says that God's grace works upon our human nature; therefore, it was almost my destiny to become a lay Catholic Evangelist and leader in the 3rd millennium. I have never been one to sit on the sidelines. I like to be on the playing field, it's in my nature, that's the way God hardwired me and all I can do is go with it!

When I retired from the Los Angeles Sheriff's Department I immediately went into a second vocation/career. The Lord recast me and remolded me into an effusive power preaching Catholic Lay Evangelist with devil-destroying theology. I know that the very reason why the Catholic Church exists is to evangelize. Evangelization is our birthright, evangelization is our missionary call, and evangelization is our most noble vocation and duty. Loving God, saving souls and slaying error is the great commission that Our Blessed Lord Jesus Christ gave us before He ascended into heaven. Every time I get behind a microphone I thank God for the opportunity because I realize that I just have a certain number of inhales and exhales left. When I am on stage evangelizing behind a podium I get pumped up, the old athlete comes out in me and I give the audience high octane muscular

Christianity. I love talking about the Lord and Holy Mother Church.

I have been blessed to be doing Catholic radio since 1998 with EWTN. I have carved out a little niche for myself as a Catholic Radio Evangelist. I generally start off my programs with this prayer: "Oh Lord open up my lips so that my mouth may proclaim your praises, Glory be to the Father and to the Son and to the Holy Spirit, as it was in the beginning is now and ever shall be world without end. Amen. Beloved in Christ, welcome to another broadcast of 'REASONS FOR FAITH,' this is the 'Holy Hour of Power.' You've just entered the 'No Sin Zone,' this is the 'Lord's Gym,' HIS PAIN IS YOUR GAIN. My name is Jesse Romero and I am your spiritual fitness trainer. I am the Latin lover of our Lord and Savior Jesus Christ and the Latin Lover of our Lady, I'm a retired L.A. Deputy Sheriff, former boxing and karate instructor, but now by the grace of God and through His election, I have been called to be a missionary Catholic lay Evangelist; I am proud to serve the Lord Jesus Christ, our Commander and Chief, and to protect the deposit of faith. I'm a hit-man for the Holy Spirit. I'm part of the God Squad, I'm part of TEAM JESUS, I'm part of the C.I.A. (Catholics In Action), I'm part of the F.B.I (Firm Believer In), I'm part of C.S.I. (Catholic's Saving Individuals), I'm part of the U.F.C. (Ultimate Faithful Catholics), I'm part of the MMA (Mother Mary's Army). The Lord Jesus Christ is the center of my life, I'm a mama's boy, I'm devoted to our Lady of Guadalupe and I'm a faithful son of the Pope, the Vicar of Christ, Alleluia! I am dynamically orthodox, I give you infectious joy and I am here to remind you to Stand Up, Stand Up, Stand Up for JESUS with your lives, your lips and your love. Now, on today's program…"

I say to people who call in, "Welcome to the Lord's Gym," because this metaphor should remind us that our faith is dynamic, we have to work at it every day just like any serious athlete does. Some of you hit your local gym almost every day to get in a work out; you should have at least the same intensity when it comes to your spiritual life. St Ignatius of Loyola called his men "athletes for Christ." I constantly tell people to "do what is good, love what is true, and listen to my Catholic radio show where I promote dynamic orthodoxy and infectious joy. Become a radioactive

Catholic and become contagious with the Gospel of Our Lord and Savior Jesus Christ."

I am known for my straight talk approach; the reason I'm so passionate is because we are living in some pretty dark days which Pope John Paul II has deemed the culture of death. I will be quite honest with you, after having grown up in the 70's and 80's where I was taught politically correct Catholicism and the social gospel of 'I'm ok, you're ok, let's hold hands now and sing Kumbaya,' I learned from experience that this nonsense doesn't work well. It left an entire generation un-catechized.

This is the 11th hour. I know too much and I'm too old to be playing silly games. What we're witnessing before our own eyes is the destruction of western civilization by our own hands as a result of secular humanism and moral relativism. We are called to be a lighthouse amidst the gathering storm. We are called to shine the light of truth upon this culture of death and put the spotlight of truth upon this forest of paganism. The new evangelization is our responsibility. If not us, then who will? If not now, then when? I am here to teach people the Catholic art of self-defense and to turn your frown upside down. When we talk about the Lord Jesus Christ we should be like lions breathing fire!

The devil (cf. Jn 8:44) is our invisible enemy who uses the unbelieving world and the disordered appetites of our flesh against us. The devil is perfectly described by way of analogy in the 1984 movie The Terminator, in one of the most memorable quotes from Kyle Reese, a soldier sent back in time to protect Sarah Connor. What Kyle Reese said about the Terminator (a cyborg made of metal surrounded by living tissue) applies perfectly to the devil and his evil ways: "You still don't get it, do you? He'll find her! That's what he does! That's ALL he does! You can't stop him! He'll wade through you, reach down her throat and pull her ***** heart out! Listen and understand. That terminator is out there. It can't be bargained with. It can't be reasoned with. It doesn't feel pity, or remorse, or fear. And it absolutely will not stop, ever, until you are dead."

Our enemy uses the world to attack us because the "whole world is in the power of the evil one" (1 Jn 5:19). He uses the triple evil of (1) the secular humanist, (2) the moral relativist, and (3) the liberal progressive carnal men who are using the power of the courts to reshape our society with a preemptive strike on

Christianity. All Christian bibles, books, crosses, symbols, ceremonies and holidays have been ordered out of the public schools. Out went Adam and Eve, in came Heather has two Mommies. Out went Easter, in came earth day. Out went collections for the poor and homeless and in came recycling and the "go green" earth worshipers. Out went Bible teachings about the immorality of homosexuality; in came the homosexuals to teach about the immorality of homophobia. Out went school prayer and in came pornography, obscenities, vulgarity and profanity. Out went boys' military haircuts and in came purple, orange and green hair Mohawks with nose, tongue and cheek piercings. Out went our Judeo Christian heritage and in came an introduction to Islam and the dogma of Darwinism. Out goes modest dress and in comes the dress code of freaks. Out goes music and the fine arts and in comes Planned Parenthood. Out goes the electives on etiquette and manners and in comes the promotion of the lesbian, gay, bisexual, and transgender lifestyles. Out went the teachings about right and wrong and in comes politically correct tolerance and moral relativism. Out went the Ten Commandments and in came condoms and birth control. Out went the parental rights of Mom and Dad and in came medical marijuana. Out went the notion of One Nation Under God and in came the study of witchcraft, vampires and totem poles. Out went any mention of the Christ and in came chaos, shootings and violence. For the sake of our children, it's time we fight back!

These are hard times for loyal Catholics. The media assaults us, our culture of death mocks us and dissenters (also called cafeteria Catholics) undermine us from within. But Holy Mother Church was founded by Jesus, upon the Rock who was Peter, and Christ promised that the gates of hell would never prevail against Her. And they haven't. The Catholic Church is the oldest institution in the western world, perhaps the entire world. The Church has been attacked from within and outside for twenty centuries. The Church has prevailed over wicked Roman Emperors and heretics: Alaric the barbarian King, Attila the Hun, Genseric the Vandal King, the Visigoth invaders, Mohammed and the Muslims, crusades which lasted 8 centuries. The corrupt kings of England, the Mongolians, the Protestant Reformers, Ivan the terrible the 1st Russian Czar, the French Revolution, Napoleon

Bonaparte, Charles Darwin, King Mwanga, The Japanese Imperialist Shogun's Tokugawa Iemitsu ("military dictators"), the Chinese Ming Dynasty, the Chinese Communist Party, Benito Mussolini, Vladimir Lenin, the Spain dictators, Joseph Stalin, Plutarco Calles, Pol Pot, Ho Chi Minh, Adolph Hitler, Mao Tse Tung, Fidel Castro, Che Guevara, Islamo Fascism, liberalism, modernism—and the Church has buried and outlasted each and every one of her enemies.

Charles Dickens wrote in his book *The Tale of Two Cities* something which describes this present darkness: These are the best of times; these are the worst of times. Yes, things look pretty bad these days, but when are you able to see farthest into the heavens, in the day or in the night? You see farther in the dark, in the night, for in the night you see the stars. Yes, we are in times of darkness, but God will give us the grace to see Him; He is our shining star through the night's darkness. The Lord is our quiet song in the storm of life. Jesus is like honey on my lips, Jesus is my melody at midnight, Jesus is that constant hymn in my heart. Jesus is my hope (1 Timothy 1:1)!

"Hope is the theological virtue by which we desire the kingdom and eternal life as our happiness placing our trust in Christ's promises and relying not on our own strength, but on the help of the grace of the Holy Spirit" (CCC 1817). I'm too blessed to be stressed, too anointed to be disappointed and if Hope were money, I'd be a millionaire. My G.P.S. is programmed for heaven, what about yours. G.P.S is not 'Global Positioning System,' it is 'God's Plan for Salvation.' Live your life with eternity in mind. Some day you gonna die bro, then where you gonna go? Here's the bottom line to my rhyme, give your life to God while you still have time!

We are the class of 33 A.D. and our class reunion is coming soon. Catholicism is 2000 years of Christian Tradition and still under the same management. What are we afraid of? We're part of TEAM JESUS and the Lord Jesus Christ is an army of ONE. Let me remind you, on Calvary, our Lord Jesus Christ bench pressed the sins of the world. Let me put this in perspective, yes we are engaged in hand to hand combat with the Culture of Death, but the Culture of Death has an expiration date (cf. Rev 21:4), and the Church is indestructible (cf. Matt 16:18).

We are the Mystical Body of Christ, we are the Church Militant, and we are TEAM JESUS. As I've preach thousands of times on radio, the Catholic Church is a TEAM. Christ is our captain and we are the members; each with a unique talent that makes us irreplaceable. The fact of the matter is this: We're engaged in a contest between two "teams" the Culture of Life versus the Culture of Death. The stakes are very high. We're not struggling to win ribbons that will fade or medals that will tarnish.

We're fighting for the hearts and souls of people! Like a football team, we have an offense and a defense. On offense, we teach and promote Christian humanism (which is the identity of man from Christ's point of view). We find effective ways to insert ourselves and our principles into society as yeast and salt. On defense, we dig in our heels and resist the onslaught of the Culture of Death. We empower every soul to push back the Culture of Death. And we keep fighting for victory until the final gun sounds or in our case, until the final trumpet sounds signaling the Second Coming of Christ! Until that time, we must do all we can to get people out of the stands and onto the playing field. And once there, to give them the equipment, strategy and coaching they need to win the contest. Your personal prayer and communal prayer are indispensable. On a practical level we must:

➢ *Reactivate our Church's pulpits so that our prophetic tongue finds its voice.*
➢ *Give parents solid catechesis in order for them to teach their children.*
➢ *Use the media and technology in order to proclaim the Gospel of Life just like the enemy has been doing for far too long.*
➢ *Empower people with apologetics in order to disarm the empty promises and false arguments of the Culture of Death. There is an expiration date to the Culture of Death (cf. Rev 21:4).*

This "Plan of Action" details the Catholic Church's game plan. The Church exists to help people fall in love with God, save souls and slay error. In this manner we help defend people from the Culture of Death. Let's go on the offensive and attack the lies spread by the Culture of Death through Catholic media and modern technology.

All Christ asks of us is that we go back to basic training and prepare ourselves for these battles which only the Catholic Church has the weapons to fight. Remember that our General is coming soon—and we want to be ready. Our Lord Jesus said, "Fear is useless, what is needed is trust...Let not your hearts be troubled." What matters is that we run the race to the finish line and fight the good fight. Many saints will be forged in the crucible (of fire) in the coming years. Make sure you are among them. Don't "go with the flow," for as the great Archbishop Fulton Sheen reminds us, "Dead bodies float downstream." More than ever we shall have to be strong in the faith. In the end we have the certainty that truth will triumph over lies, light over darkness and good over evil. So stand firm Catholics and rush to the battle lines with Jesus in your heart, a rosary in one hand and a bible in the other. No matter what happens, no matter how this battle turns out, we know that we win! No matter what political party is in power at any given point in time, in the end those that remain faithful to Jesus Christ win.

WE WIN!

Don't Quit, Never Surrender and No Excuses

A priest friend/mentor of mine always reminds me that a man has a Mission, an Identity and a Journey. Their natural Mission is to be leaders, protectors and providers. Their supernatural mission is to be Priest's, Prophets and Kings. His identity is to progress from the 1) Beloved Son, to the 2) Loyal Brother, to the 3) Vital Man and in his adulthood he moves from the 4) Devoted Husband to the 5) Strong Father and finally to the 6) Veteran Sage. His Journey is to lead his family in virtue by example and thereby lead them to Heaven. Jesus Christ our role model is the Lamb of God and the lion of Judah. Every woman wants to be a lamb by their sacrificial love and she wants a lion to lead them.

Do not be afraid, remember the words of Emperor Constantine before the battle of Milvian Bridge, he saw the Cross in the sky along with the words, "Hoc Signo Victor Eris" (By this Sign we will conquer), he believed and he did.

NO EXCUSES . . . The next time you feel like God cannot use you, just remember:

NOAH was a drunk.
ABRAHAM was too old.
METHUSELAH was even older (969 years old)

ISAAC was a daydreamer.

JACOB was a liar.

LEAH was not very pretty.

JOSEPH was abused.

MOSES had a stuttering problem.

GIDEON was afraid.

SAMPSON had long hair, and he was a womanizer too.

RAHAB was a prostitute.

JEREMIAH and TIMOTHY were too young.

DAVID had an affair and he was a murderer.

ELIJAH was suicidal.

ISAIAH preached naked.

JONAH ran from God.

NAOMI was a widow.

JOB went bankrupt.

JOHN THE BAPTIST ate bugs.

PETER denied Christ.

THE DISCIPLES fell asleep while praying.

MARTHA worried about everything.

MARY MAGDALENE was a prostitute.

THE SAMARITAN WOMAN was divorced more than once.

ZACCHEUS was too small.

PAUL was too religious.

TIMOTHY had an ulcer.

And LAZARUS was DEAD!!

So, no more excuses. God is waiting for your full potential. After all, you are not the message. You are just the messenger!

The New Evangelization is our responsibility: If not us, than who will? If not now, then when? Now go and be the voice of the New Evangelization. Go out and evangelize, reconcile, celebrate and pray hard because life is short! May the Lord bless you, keep you safe, may His shine his face upon you and be gracious to you, and may the Lord lift you up and give you His peace. Amen.

MEN OF THE CATECHISM

MARLON DE LA TORRE

DEACON HAROLD BURKE-SIVERS

FR. STEVE GRUNOW

Theological Manhood

MARLON DE LA TORRE, MA, M.ED.

Our Relationship with the Triune God

Then God said; let us make man in our image and likeness . . . so he created man in his own image. . . Gen 1:26-27

If you were to ask any man walking down the street if he saw himself as an image of God, you might get a blank stare or no physical response at all. Unfortunately, this type of question is not often pondered by men, let alone embraced. Man's calculated disengagement of living outside the realm of God reflects how he looks from himself and at himself. A relationship with God can be the most distant thing on a man's mind.

One of the tendencies of man after the fall was establishing a relationship with himself rather than God. Thus, when we read in Sacred Scripture the actions of Noah (Gen 6), Abraham (Gen 12), and Jacob (Gen 28) for example, their intention after openness to God's words reflects a willingness to embrace God in their lives through prayer, sacrifice and worship. These characteristics express a willingness to forgo themselves and embrace something more powerful than them.

The Trinity offers us an opportunity to see God's love repeatedly, not only through our very own creation, but through the culmination of the redemptive and salvific works of the Son of God, Jesus Christ. Jesus Christ the Second Person of the Blessed Trinity, distinct in person but one in nature (Divine) reveals the Father's plan for all of humanity (I Jn 1:1-4). God desires for all his children to be in communion with Him if we so choose. Our very nature as men created in the image and likeness of God reflects a call and duty to worship God, but to also represent him in a manner worthy of the Gospel set forth by the Son Jesus Christ: And one of them, a lawyer, asked him a question, to test him. "Teacher, which is the greatest commandment in the law? And he said to him, "You shall love the Lord your God with all of your heart, and with all of your soul, and with all your mind. This is the great and first commandment. And the second is like it. You shall love your neighbor as yourself. On these two commandments depend all the law and the prophets." (Mt 22:35-40) Also see: Ex 20:3; Deut 5:7.

The greatest commandment to love reflects the call of our Father in Heaven to love in order to dispel sin. Sin, by definition, is an act of self-love versus an act of love toward others. Man's vocation is linked to the revelation of God in the blessed Trinity. His (our) vocation is to make God manifest by acting in conformity with his creation "in the image and likeness of God." (CCC 2085) If we are true men of the Gospel, then our actions are ordered to this visible reality found in the Trinity aptly revealed in every Crucifix we encounter.

Our nature as men created in God's image reflects the love he has for all humanity. Specifically speaking, we are men because we of God's divine will. We are called to align ourselves with God and His Church. Our masculinity depends on this alignment. When we decide to deviate from it from this gift, we pervert the very nature of being a man in image and likeness of our Father in Heaven.

Men tend to forget the reason or essence, so to speak, of why they're men. This is due to a perversion I alluded to earlier when man veers off the track with his identity. Though different in every way from woman anatomically, emotionally, spiritually etc. man has received a unique quality aimed at protecting, gathering, providing and leading a flock with great care i.e. prudence, wisdom, and charity. Man is called to serve as a spiritual head in communion with his bride. He is a reflection of the Trinity; it is his very nature to impart the image of God toward others, especially his own family. This is the essence I speak of. Man must reflect the love revealed by the Father in our creation.

We read in *Genesis* 2:19 that man received dominion over all the beasts of the earth, even naming them. This responsibility granted by God reflects a gift bestowed on man to take care of these gifts. And, in these gifts, man is called to exercise his natural role as a father and a husband as freely given by God. These characteristics unique to man alone as father and husband reflect the love God has for man in this role: Being in the image of God the human individual possesses the dignity of the human person, who is not something, but someone. He is capable of self-knowledge, of self-possession and of freely giving himself and entering into communion with other persons. And he is called by grace to a covenant with his Creator to offer him a response of faith and love that ho other creature can give in his stead. (CCC 357)

Man's vocation rests on his willingness to see himself as a child of God and in turn reflect this characteristic towards others. Fidelity is an attribute we can apply to man's responsibility to profess the kingdom of God in word and deed. Christ reminds us to be cautious of the things that come out of us that are not of God: Hear and understand: not what goes into the mouth that defiles a man, but what comes out of the mouth, this defiles a man. (Mt 15:11)

Our character as men is intrinsically linked to the Trinitarian life by nature of our created order in the image and likeness of God. Our manhood so to speak is called to exhibit a sense of authority that embraces Christ crucified to the point of offering ourselves as Christ did for us. Man occupies a unique place in creation: (I) he is "in the image of God"; (II) in his own nature he unites the spiritual and material worlds; (III) he is created "male and female"; (IV) God established him in his friendship. (CCC 355)

Manhood and the Creed
But if a blind man leads a blind man, both will fall into a pit. Mt 15:14

Men can be stubborn mules so to speak when it comes to proving a point we may not have the upper hand on. I know, because I'm one of those stubborn fools that falls flat on his face when it comes to these types of situations. My own concupiscence gets in the way because of my stubbornness to prove a point. Ultimately it's my own fault for not conceding. This is ever more visible when I converse with my wife and a topic comes up where we have differing views and both of us are standing our ground on our personal view of the topic. Right or wrong, one is right and one is wrong. The challenge here is conceding to my wife when I'm wrong, which is often the case!

A man's masculinity by nature is creedal. All of God's children are created with a natural desire to assent towards a creed. However, for the sake of this resource, I am particularly concentrating on man's innate being to believe and lead. The creedal nature I allude to reflects a man's natural ability to assert his authority, force, or position in any situation. The visible action often results in a subtle, moderate, or aggressive approach to a situation. In other words, our masculine nature dictates that everything depends on us to fix. The problem with this is that when we don't have a clear direction on what or why we are doing something, we tend to "fall into the pit" so to speak. Christ reminds us of the need to "surrender" ourselves from our own human desires: If any man would come after me, let him deny himself and take up his cross and follow me. For whoever would save his life will lose it. And who ever loses his life for my sake will find it. For what will it profit a man, if he gains the whole world and forfeits his life? For the Son of Man is to come with his angels in the glory of his Father, and then he will repay every man for what he has done. Truly, I say to you, there are some standing here who will not taste death before they see the Son of man coming in his kingdom. (Mt 17:24-28)

Man's response to God is a response to His invitation to be in communion with Him. One way by which we can respond to God's call more faithfully is through the establishment of a creed. To us, it appears that God has spent a lifetime establishing a creed we can all follow. Case in point, Abrams blessing from Melchizedek (Gen 14:17-17) centered on a feast consisting of unleavened bread and pure wine, also His covenant with Moses and the establishment of the Rule of Faith, i.e. the Ten Commandments. Behind these two examples lies the placement of an action to be followed and believed because it comes from God. These actions reveal a freely given way of "being" if we so choose. In other words, what we have received from God is a way of life if we desire this life, this intimate union, with Him.

Hence the *Apostles Creed* serves as the foundation of our response of faith to spread the Gospel. As mentioned earlier, man's natural tendency is to keep to his own position. This can distract him from following the Creedal way of life set forth by Christ (Mt 28:17-20; Acts 2:37-42). The *Creed* expresses man's desire to pledge what he believes is revealed by God and His Church: This synthesis of faith was not made to accord with human opinions, but rather what was of the greatest importance was gathered from all the Scriptures, to present the one teaching of the faith in its entirety. And just as the mustard seed contains a great number of branches in a tiny grain, so too this summary of faith encompassed in a few words the whole knowledge of the true religion contained in the Old and New Testaments. (St. Cyril of Jerusalem, CCC 186)

A man's affirmation is not with himself but with God. Belief in the *Creed* allows man not to fall "into the pit" but instead lead others from suffering the same fate. As men, our relationship with Christ should be distinctive (CCC 202). It carries a certain personification that it's not about what we think or believe to be true, it is how we freely embrace God's revelation of love to us and in turn we embrace and share that love with others. This is why when St. Peter's asks Christ to explain this parable of falling "into the pit", Jesus responds: Do you not see that whatever goes into the mouth passes into the stomach, and so passes on? But what comes out of the stomach proceeds from the heart, and this defiles a man. For out of the heart come evil thoughts, murder, adultery, fornication, theft, false witness, slander. These are what defile a man . . ." (Mt 15:17-20)

The *Creed* lays the foundation of centering ourselves to and in Christ. St. Paul reminds Timothy to "guard what has been entrusted to you (1 Tim 6:20) in relation to maintaining fidelity to what Christ has handed down. St. Jude reflects the same point that the deposit of faith i.e. the *Creed* has been delivered once and for all (Jude 1:3). These examples reflect the *Creed* as the stem by which the flowering of faith blossoms into an authentic manhood that looks at Christ rather than the self. As men we are called to walk freely in Christ so as to not "fall into the pit." The simple words: I believe in one God the Father the almighty creator of Heaven and of Earth, firmly establishes our duty and responsibility as men.

Man's Battle with Sin

No one can serve two masters; for either he will hate the one and love the other, or he will be devoted to the one and despise the other. You cannot serve God and mammon. (Mt 6:24) The *Catechism* tells us that man is called to perform good acts (CCC 1749). If this is true, then what we just covered on the *Creed*, the Deposit of Faith, makes clear sense. The performance of a good act requires the development of a sound moral conscience. It compels man to do what is good and to avoid evil. (CCC 1776)

Our tendency as men is to draw on the notion that we can handle it ourselves. This may explain why a husband would never think of asking for directions when lost on the road even though his wife had charitably told him to several times to "please ask for directions," knowing that he would not even think of asking for directions. This light hearted example illustrates our battle with sin. Man has a free will as a result of the fall to choose good or bad acts. Every waking moment all humanity is faced with the freedom to perform an act based on their conscience whether it's properly formed or not. The morality of the human act is based on the object, the intent, and the circumstance (CCC 1750). These criteria are a direct result of the freedoms we possess to perform these acts. St. Paul shows us how God will deal with wicked men: And since they did not see fit to acknowledge God, God gave them up to a base mind and to improper conduct. They were filled with all the manner of wickedness, evil, covetousness, malice...full of envy, murder, strife, deceit, malignity...gossips, slanderers, haters of God, insolent, haughty, boastful, inventors of evil, disobedient to parents, foolish faithless, heartless, ruthless. Though they know God's decree that those who do such things deserve to die, they not only do them but approve those who practice them. (Rom 1:28-32)

St. Paul reminds us of the freedoms we possess and that our actions have consequences, especially when we know they're wrong. This is where sin rears its ugly head and offers an alternative to love yourself before ever loving God. Simply put, sin is a rejection of God's love. It is an offense against reason, truth, and right conscience; it is a failure in genuine love for God and neighbor caused by a perverse attachment to certain goods. (CCC 1849) Man's actions must reflect a willingness to show love others before anyone else. Man is naturally built to be a caretaker. Thus when a man abuses the sexual integrity of a woman for pure sexual pleasure, the entire picture of the Trinity, the *Creed*, and the Deposit of Faith is thrown out the window. This is how powerful our actions against Christ and others can affect our soul.

Where sin abounded, grace abounded all the more. (Rom 5:20) The masculine spirit of Catholicism reflects a desire to sin no more. This comes from a free desire to seek grace from Christ clearly seen in the sacramental life of the Church. Why would Christ have established the sacraments if not to make His presence clearly known? In many ways, when we deviate from Christ we automatically take on a Prodigal Son (Lk 15:11-32) mentality. For one split moment our sinful actions reflect a "love me" attitude. All of us are called to make resolutions not to sin. And if we do sin, then seek a proper penance to sin no more (Mt 18:21-22; Jn 20:20-22).

A true Catholic masculine spirit exemplifies a desire to die to self and embrace Christ in everything we do (Jn 3:30). The *Catechism* aptly places our duty as men to avoid sin and embrace Christ in this way: Penance requires the sinner to endure all things willingly, be contrite of heart, confess with the lips, and practice complete humility and fruitful satisfaction. Among the penitent's acts contrition occupies first place. Contrition is "sorrow of the soul and detestation for the sin committed, together with the resolution not to sin again." When it arises from a love by which God is loved above all else, contrition is called "perfect" (contrition of charity). Such contrition remits venial sins; it also obtains forgiveness of mortal sins if it includes the firm resolution to have recourse to sacramental confession as soon as possible. (CCC 1456-1452)

St. Augustine reminds us: Whoever confesses his sins... is already working with God. God indicts your sins; if you also indict them, you are joined with God. Man and sinner are, so to speak, two realities: when you hear "man"—this is what God has made; when you hear "sinner"—this is what man himself has made. Destroy what you have made, so that God may save what he has made.... When you begin to abhor what you have made, it is then that your good works are beginning, since you are accusing yourself of your evil works. The beginning of good works is the confession of evil works. You do the truth and come to the light. (CCC 1458)

Active Warriors in the Vineyard

The following tools aim to help any man who desires to be a better model of Catholic masculinity in Christ's vineyard. Our charge as men of Christ is to foster an authentic masculinity that exudes the character of man as a protector, care-giver, guide, and spiritual head of the household. This requires a two-fold response to be a man of God and a child of God.

A Father's Moral Resolution

St. Paul tells us: "I do not understand my own actions. For I do not do what I want, but I do the very thing I hate." (Rom 7:15) St. Paul provides a great springboard for any father desiring to be a better moral witness to their children. "Don't do the things you hate; that would provide a negative example to your children." Sounds easier said than done. However, when put to the test, watching what you say or do can prove to be quite challenging, especially if it's habitual. The goal of any parent is to be a model of holiness to their children, in particular how to establish and live a personal relationship with Jesus Christ. St. John reminds of this simple plan; I must decrease, He must increase (Jn 3:30).

So, how do you begin to gauge your moral compass for the sake of your children? The following biblical principles offer us "dads" a glimpse on exercising authentic moral masculinity that I believe our children so desperately need and desire.

1. *"Always be ready to give an explanation for the hope that is in you . . ." (1 Pt 3:15-17) Children view their fathers as a barometer of how things will turn out that day by their demeanor towards themselves and those around them. St. Peter stresses the value of hope in a catechetical sense as the chief means of witnessing the Gospel of Jesus Christ to others.*

2. *"O Lord, open my lips, and mouth shall show forth your praise." (Psalm 51:15) Many of us use the strength and depth of our voices to command authority, respect, and discipline from our children. However the very gift we perceive as a great asset can potentially be a deficit. I firmly believe our fatherly language must exhibit a depth that commands respect. But it must not be abused nor used as a weapon. The fatherly language I just mentioned must reecho Christ in our communication with our children.*

3. *Ask it will be given to you, seek and you will find; knock and it will be opened to you. (Mt 7:7) The virtue of humility goes a long way in parenting, especially when our children correct our faults. Great character befalls a man who understands his limitations and receives fraternal correction.*

4. *For what does it prophet a man if he gains the whole world and loses or forfeits himself? (Lk 9:25 My children have never asked me how much money I make or what does the family financial portfolio look like. They merely ask me what time will I be home so "we" can play. This simple question helps me understand the desires of the world cannot supersede my role as a father and husband to my wife and children.*

Biblical Manhood

DEACON HAROLD BURKE-SIVERS

There is no doubt that by prayerfully reading the Bible, men can have a deeply meaningful and profound encounter with God the Father. Men can personally experience Christ, the Word who became flesh, through a deeper appreciation and better understanding of how to read the Bible as a Catholic man, why this is important, and how a man uses the Bible for moral guidance. Being open to the Holy Spirit, the hope is that you will take your Bible off the shelf and start reading it every day that you will begin to see yourself and your life in the pages of Scripture and then use this knowledge to grow spiritually as a man of God.

God is the author of Scripture because the Holy Spirit is its inspiration and guide; it is God telling His story. He uses human authors as instruments to communicate the truth of divine revelation, that is, how God reveals Himself in salvation history for the purpose of inviting us into intimate, personal, loving and life-giving communion with Him.

"In order to discover the sacred authors' intention, the reader must take into account the conditions of their time and culture, the literary genres in use at that time, and the modes of feeling, speaking and narrating then current."[i] This is an important point. The reason why some passages in the Bible (especially in the *Old Testament*) appear confusing is that we are trying to read it with a twenty-first century mindset without recognizing how someone within the time period would have understood what is being said.

Let's imagine, for example, we are in the year 2101. A group of archeologists are digging at a recently discovered twentieth century actor's theatre in San Francisco that was destroyed by an earthquake in 1989. Buried in the rubble, they find a VCR tape. The very excited scientists carefully excavate the tape and bring it to a nearby museum that has a working VCR player. After painstakingly repairing and restoring as much of the tape as they could, the archeologists load the VCR tape into the machine and push "play." The tape is grainy and somewhat choppy but they are able to decipher some of it. It's a conversation between two actors. One of the actors is heard saying to the other, "Get out there and break a leg!" The scientists are horrified. One of them writes an article about the VCR artifact stating that the tape clearly reveals that twentieth century men were barbarians.

The above example illustrates the importance of literary form, genre, syntax, etc. when attempting to read and understand Sacred Scripture. Like the archeologists who viewed the VCR tape with a twenty-second century mindset, thereby not appreciating the fact that the twentieth century colloquial expression "break a leg" actually means "good luck," those who read Scripture without understanding the proper literary and historical context (which leads to the deeper, spiritual meaning) will not understand and, consequently, misinterpret what they are reading. This is why the Catholic Church has a "both-and" approach to understanding and interpreting the Bible known as the four "senses" of Scripture.

The first is the Literal (also called the Literal-Historical) sense. "The literal sense is the meaning conveyed by the words of Scripture and discovered by exegesis, following the rules of sound interpretation."[ii] This does not mean we are to necessarily read every verse in the Bible and interpret it literally but, rather, to use sound interpretive methods to determine what the human author intended to teach and have his audience understand. The literal sense is about getting inside of the author's mind in such a way that we really understand what he's getting at. This is the typical method employed by and used in biblical commentaries on Scripture.

The next three senses are grouped together and are known as the Spiritual senses of Scripture. The spiritual senses are fuller and deeper than the literal where we seek to discover what the Divine Author is intending to say through the Bible. They are called the allegorical, tropological, and anagogical senses.[iii]

The allegorical sense allows us to acquire a more profound understanding of Biblical events by recognizing their significance in light of Jesus Christ. The crossing of the Red Sea in Exodus 14, for example, where the Israelites escaped from slavery in Egypt, is seen allegorically as a precursor to baptism where, by His death and resurrection, Jesus frees us from slavery to sin and death.

The tropological or moral sense points out how we ought to live and act justly. The Ten Commandments in the Old Testament

(Ex 20) and the Beatitudes in the *New Testament* (Matt 5) would be examples of the moral sense of Scripture.

In the anagogical sense, we can view realities and events in the Bible in terms of their eternal significance leading us toward our true homeland, the heavenly Jerusalem. These passages in Scripture foreshadow what heaven is like. Jesus, for example, compares our experience in heaven to a wedding feast (Matt 22 and Rev 19).

Knowing the senses of Scripture and why they are important are critical to a proper Catholic understanding of the Bible. The better we know Scripture the more we can see ourselves on every page. God's story is also our story. The ultimate goal of understanding God's revelation in Scripture goes hand-in-hand with the ultimate goal of exegesis: personal transformation and intimate union with our Lord Jesus Christ.

The question now becomes: how do I see myself as a man of God in the Bible? Using the sense of Scripture outlined above, we will examine the foundational principles of an authentic Catholic male spirituality rooted in the *Book of Genesis* and Saint Paul's *Letter to the Ephesians.*

The first man of the Bible—literally—is Adam. In *Genesis* 2:15 we read, "The Lord God took the man and put him in the Garden of Eden to till it and keep it." The word for "till" (abad in Hebrew) means a work in the form of service. The word for "keep" (shamar in Hebrew) means to guard, protect, and defend. Adam, then, is not simply a gardener but a steward who receives his mission and calling from God: to serve, protect and defend everything that the Lord has entrusted to him.

God then gives man his only commandment, "You may freely eat of every tree of the garden; but of the tree of the knowledge of good and evil you shall not eat, for in the day that you eat of it you shall die."[iv] What is so special about the tree and why is it in the garden? First, we see that God created man with freedom and self-determination rooted in both a healthy respect for his limits before God and a humble appreciation of the infinite chasm between God's authority and his own. Man's existence is a gift from God and to use our freedom to contravene God's holy will would result in "death" (mavet in Hebrew), in cutting ourselves off from the life of God.

Second, we see that God's command is specific to "the tree of the knowledge of good and evil." The word for "knowledge" used here (yada in Hebrew) refers to knowledge that is gained by personal experience, that is, you come to "know" something through your experience of it. If you tell a child, for example, not to touch the hot stove, the child may use his or her free will and make a choice to touch the stove anyway. They now "know" what "hot" means! The same is true in the Garden of Eden. The tree itself is not evil since everything that God creates is good. God's warning to man expressed His desire that man use his free will to remain in loving and life-giving communion with Him. He did not want man to use his free will to experience or "know" separation from His divine life—sin and death.

"Then the LORD God said, "It is not good that the man should be alone; I will make him a helper fit for him."[v] Why is the man's solitary existence not a good thing? In his Original Solitude,[vi] man realizes that he is superior to all God's creatures, he is self-aware (he can know himself), and he can know God. Man is also made in the image and likeness of God (Gen 1:27) who exists as one God in a communion of three Persons: Father, Son and Holy Spirit. Man, therefore, is created to exist within a family, in a communion of persons who are three but one: fathers, mothers and children.[vii] Man makes no sense by himself and so God creates a "helpmate" fit for him.

The Hebrew word for "helpmate" is ezerkenegdo. The root of the word ezer means "power" and "strength." Combined with kenegdo ("opposite to" or "corresponding to"), the phrase was often used in a military setting to denote one who stands opposite (parallel to) the other and who surrounds, protects, aids, helps, and supports, especially in battle. So God created a woman in the same Original Solitude as the man (she is also superior to all God's creatures, is self-aware and can know God) but has her own gifts from God that complete and perfect the gifts of the man. They are to battle sin and death … together.

"So the Lord God caused a deep sleep to fall upon the man, and while he slept took one of his ribs and closed up its place with flesh; and the rib which the Lord God had taken from the man he made into a woman and brought her to the man."[viii] When God created woman, he did not start over with another lump of clay (Gen 2:7). Rather, he takes a rib from the side of man to create the woman. Why a rib? If God used a bone from the lower extremities, she would be less than him. If God used a bone from the upper part of the body, she would be greater than him. The Lord uses a rib from the man's side to show that she is equal to him, equal right from the beginning. Equal but not the same.

This is an extremely important point. We live in a culture today that insists "equality" and "sameness" are identical, expressing itself in the sentiment, "In order to be equal you have to be the same." This fails the litmus credibility test since there exists within the complimentarity of men and women a fundamental and intrinsic unity. In other words, men and women are equal in dignity but are different physically, emotionally and spiritually. The gifts from God that are unique and special to men compliment and perfect the unique and special gifts of women. To be created and loved by God is not enough; what matters to us beyond existence is to be loved by another person. The overflow of God's infinite love is continued and perfected by the creative power of human love between a man and a woman in the covenant relationship of marriage.

"Then the man said, 'This at last is bone of my bones and flesh of my flesh; she shall be called Woman, because she was taken out of Man.'"[ix]Here, the man acknowledges the splendor and magnificence of his wife. How so? Semitic languages like Hebrew and Aramaic do not have superlatives, that is, they do not have words that express an idea or concept to the highest degree, words like "greatest," "best" and "most." Superlative ideas are typically expressed in two ways in those languages. They would either repeat something three times[x]or they would use a prepositional phrase.[xi]When the man says his wife is "bone of my bones and flesh of my flesh", he is saying that she is "the greatest of my bone" and "the greatest of my flesh ... she is the greatest part of who I am, she is my equal." By calling her woman (ishshah in Hebrew), he acknowledges her unique, God-given gifts that compliment his manhood (ish in Hebrew).

"Therefore a man leaves his father and his mother and cleaves to his wife, and they become one flesh."[xii]The verse indicates that a man's relationship with his wife (and vice versa) supersedes all previous relationships, including that of parents, and that the conjugal union of a man and a woman occurs within the covenant relationship of marriage. This is particularly important today where marriage is being redefined as a contractual relationship between people who love each other. So what is the difference between a contract and a covenant?

All throughout the Bible, when God wanted to establish a relationship with His people, he established a covenant. A contract is an exchange of goods, "This is yours and this is mine." It is an agreement between two parties that can be dissolved if one party is dissatisfied. A covenant is exchange of persons, "I am yours and you are mine." In a covenant, you make a complete gift of yourself to someone, and that someone makes a complete gift of himself or herself back to you in an outpouring of life-giving love—in love that is free, faithful, total and fruitful—that endures for the entire life of the spouses.[xiii] It is a love that gives everything and holds nothing back. This is the love of Christ on the Cross, a love that lasts forever.

"And the man and his wife were both naked, and were not ashamed."[xiv]They were not ashamed of each other because they are looking at each other through God's eyes; what they see is what God sees. This is God's plan. So what happened?

In *Genesis* 3, Satan attacks the family, going after the woman first. Why her? "In God's eternal plan, woman is the one in whom the order of love in the created world of persons takes first root."[xv]Women are the heart of love and have a special relationship with the Holy Spirit that men do not. By their very nature, all women are mothers (either physical or spiritual) because they share an intimacy with the Holy Spirit as life-bearers and life-givers. By targeting the woman, Satan is trying to destroy the family by separating the loving and life-giving dimensions of covenant relationship that flows from the heart of God Himself.

In the Garden, the man's job is to serve, protect and defend all that God had entrusted to him, most especially and above all else, his wife. Instead, he stands there are does nothing while Satan destroys his spouse. Even worse, we men today not only continue to stand by and do nothing, we are actually helping the devil to destroy our women through abortion, contraception, pornography and sterilization. The separation of love and life has created a culture of death.

Why did this happen? Prior to the Fall, the consciences of the man and his wife were directed toward their ultimate end: the Beatific Vision, life forever in heaven with God. Satan, through his lies and deceptions, forms the consciences of our First Parents away from God and toward themselves. Sadly, he has been using the same technique over and over again, millennium after millennium that continues to destroy the hearts, minds and lives of those who seek life-giving communion with God. Exactly how does he do it?

Let's say your favorite football team only has one play in their playbook. How many games would they win? The answer, of course, is none because every time they touch the ball the other team knows what play they're going to run. There is no way your team can win. It's the same with Satan. He only has one play in his playbook but we keep losing! Here's how it works.

Satan's first words to the woman are in the form of a question: "Did God say, 'You shall not eat of any tree of the garden'?" (Gen 3:1). The purpose of this question is to plant the seeds of confusion and doubt in her mind in order to form her conscience away from God and to question His authority. Her answer reveals that she is, in fact, confused: "We may eat of the fruit of the trees of the garden; but God said, 'You shall not eat of the fruit of the tree which is in the midst of the garden, neither shall you touch it, lest you die'" (Gen 3:2-3). If we look back at *Genesis* 2:16-17, God commands not to eat the fruit of the tree, He never said anything about touching it. In her confusion, the woman puts words into God's mouth that He did not say. Satan then capitalizes on the last part of her answer regarding the consequence for choosing self over God—death: "You will not die. For God knows that when you eat of it your eyes will be opened, and you will be like God, knowing good and evil" (Gen 3:4-5). Satan lies to her about the meaning of death and tempts her with the proposition that she does not need God at all; that by eating the tree's fruit she can become her own god.

"So when the woman saw that the tree was good for food, and that it was a delight to the eyes, and that the tree was to be desired to make one wise, she took of its fruit and ate; and she also gave some to her husband, and he ate" (Gen 3:6). The woman's husband is finally mentioned although he has been there the entire time. His silence is deafening and confirms his complicity in disobeying God's commandment. The verse does not imply that the woman tempted her husband into sinning, as is sometimes thought, but that he was a willing participant with his wife in introducing sin into the world. He was supposed to protect and defend her but he did not, and we are still living with the consequences of that decision today.

How do we get ourselves back on track as faithful and steadfast men of God? This is where our Lord Jesus Christ and Saint Paul come in. In *Ephesians* 5:21-33, Saint Paul juxtaposes the relationship between a husband and wife in the marriage covenant with the relationship between Christ and the Church. These verses lay the foundation for an authentic male spirituality ensconced in the image of the crucified Christ.

Saint Paul frames this particular set of verses in Ephesians around the theme of equality between a husband and his wife. *Ephesians* 5:21 emphasizes mutual subjection ("Be subject to one another out of reverence for Christ")while *Ephesians* 5:31 quotes directly from *Genesis* 2:24, emphasizing the one-flesh union in marriage ("For this reason a man shall leave his father and mother and be joined to his wife, and the two shall become one flesh"). With these bookends firmly established, Saint Paul explores the nature of covenant relationship in Christ through the lenses of sacramental marriage.

Ephesians 5:22-24 says, "Wives, be subject to your husbands, as to the Lord. For the husband is the head of the wife as Christ is the head of the church, his body, and is himself its Savior. As the church is subject to Christ, so let wives also be subject in everything to their husbands." These verses can be grossly misinterpreted without understanding the literal sense of Scripture. The word for "subject to" in Greek is hupotasso, a military term for arranging troop divisions under the command and mission of a leader. So wives are to place themselves under their husband's mission just as the Church places herself under the mission of Christ her spouse. What is the husband's mission? "Husbands, love your wives, as Christ loved the church and gave himself up for her" (Eph 5:25). A husband's mission is imitate the crucified Christ, to give his life and die every day to himself so that he can live for his wife and children just as Christ the Bridegroom gave his life for his Bride, the Church.

Every man is called to be the chief servant of his family, whether he serves as a husband and father in the domestic church (the church of the home), as a parish priest in persona Christi (in the person of Christ) in service to the Church on earth, or as a young man who serves as an example of sanctity and virtue within society as he discerns God's will for his life.[xvi]Our Lord himself teaches us by his example, "For the Son of man also came not to be served but to serve, and to give his life as a ransom for many"[xvii]and "He who is greatest among you shall be your servant; whoever exalts himself will be humbled, and whoever humbles himself will be exalted."[xviii]Our spirituality as men must flow from the Sacred Heart of Jesus and his call to live the Gospel with both fervor and humility. Humility does not mean thinking less of ourselves, it means thinking of ourselves less. Humility means making our relationship with Jesus the single most important relationship in our lives.

If we are to be true men of God, we must willingly and lovingly lay down our lives in service to our Brides bearing witness to the awesome power and testimony of the crucified Christ. We must have the courage to say with Saint Paul, "I have been crucified with Christ; it is no longer I who live, but Christ who lives in me; and the life I now live in the flesh I live by faith in the Son of God, who loved me and gave himself for me."[xix]When men pick up their Cross and follow Christ, they unite their sufferings to his Passion, receive everlasting life from his death, and draw our strength his weakness. "My grace is sufficient for you, for my power is made perfect in weakness,'" Saint Paul says, and "I will all the more gladly boast of my weaknesses, that the power of Christ may rest upon me. For the sake of Christ, then, I am content with weaknesses, insults, hardships, persecutions, and calamities; for when I am weak, then I am strong."[xx]Being vulnerable before the Lord is a sign of strength, not weakness. The gift of vulnerability means emptying ourselves before the Eucharist Christ, in complete surrender to the will of God, so that the Lord can fill us with his life.

There is so much more that could be said. I hope that this brief journey into biblical manhood has whetted your appetite for more. I encourage you to attend your parish bible study or join your local Catholic men's group to continue your journey in faith by understanding of how God reveals Himself to us as men in His Word. I encourage you to look at the lives of other Biblical men like David,[xxi]Solomon,[xxii] Joshua,[xxiii] Saint Joseph, and the Prodigal Son. The sooner we begin to appreciate the great gift we have been given in Sacred Scripture and begin living the mission of service to our families—when we begin participate deeply and personally in the Fatherhood of God—the faster we will arrive at a civilization of love and a culture of life rooted in the transforming power of the Father's endless mercy and love.

---

[i] *Catechism of the Catholic Church*, no.110.

[ii] *Catechism of the Catholic Church*, no.116.

[iii] See *Catechism of the Catholic Church*, no.117.

[iv] Genesis 2:16-17. All Scripture quotations (with the exceptions of the Psalms) are taken from the Catholic Edition of the Revised Standard Version of the Bible (1965-66). Used with permission.

[v] Genesis 2:18.

[vi] "Original Solitude" is a term used by Blessed John Paul II in his *Theology of the Body*.

[vii] The spiritual equivalent would be bridegroom (the priest), bride (the Church), and children (humanity).

[viii] Genesis 2:21-22.

[ix] Genesis 2:23.

[x] See Isaiah 6:3, "And one called to another and said: "Holy, holy, holy is the Lord of hosts; the whole earth is full of his glory" and Revelation 4:8, "And the four living creatures, each of them with six wings, are full of eyes all round and within, and day and night they never cease to sing, "Holy, holy, holy, is the Lord God Almighty, who was and is and is to come!" By repeating "holy" three times, biblical authors show that the highest glory and honor belong to God alone.

[xi] See Revelation 19:16, "On his robe and on his thigh he has a name inscribed, King of kings and Lord of lords" and 1 Timothy 6:15, "this will be made manifest at the proper time by the blessed and only Sovereign, the King of kings and Lord of lords ..." By utilizing a preposition, both authors show that Jesus Christ is the greatest of all kings and the Lord of all Lords.

[xii] Genesis 2:24.

[xiii] "The sacrament of Matrimony can be regarded in two ways: first in the making and then in its permanent state. For it is a sacrament like to that of the Eucharist, which not only while it is being conferred, but also while it remains, is a sacrament; for as long as the married parties are alive, so long is their union a sacrament of Christ and his Church." Peter J. Elliott, Rev. *What God Has Joined . . . The Sacramentality of Marriage*, 112, citing Pius XI, *CastiConnubii*, no.110, citing St. Robert Bellarmine, *De controversiis*, Tom. III, *op. cit.*, cap. vi, p.628.

[xiv] Genesis 2:25.

[xv] Pope John Paul II, *Mulieris Dignitatem*, Apostolic Letter, Vatican Translation (Boston: Pauline Books and Media, 1988), no.29.

[xvi] Ephesians 5:26-27: " ... that he might sanctify her, having cleansed her by the washing of water with the word, that he might present the church to himself in splendor, without spot or wrinkle or any such thing, that she might be holy and without blemish."

[xvii] Mark 10:45. See also Matthew 20:28.

[xviii] Matthew 23:11-12. See also Mark 9:35.

[xix] Galatians 2:20.

[xx] 2 Corinthians 12:9-10.

[xxi] 1 Samuel 16:1, 6-13; 1 Samuel 17:4-11, 19-54; 2 Samuel 11; 2 Samuel 12: 1-14; and 1 Kings 2: 1-4.

[xxii] 1 Kings 3: 5, 7-12.

[xxiii] Joshua 1:5-9, 16-18 and Joshua 24:14-15.

Sacramental Manhood

FR. STEVE GRUNOW

In 1983, Leo Steinberg's book *The Sexuality of Christ in Renaissance Art and Modern Oblivion* was published. The title alone is enough to capture considerable attention, let alone the thesis and the content. The purpose of Steinberg's research was to demonstrate that many of the Renaissance artists were willing to display, without embarrassment or hesitation, the fact that the Lord Jesus is male. This point might seem to some to be so obvious that a scholarly dissertation on the subject is something to laugh at—another example of a sheltered academic with too much time on his hands exalting a banal observation to ultimate concern. But let's think about it. Survey in your mind most popular representations of the Lord Jesus, many of which are given sacral significance in our churches, other than the placement of facial hair on the face of Christ, how many of these images really depict the Lord as distinctly male? The long robe, slender physique, softened features that are often employed by artists so as to evoke accessibility also communicate a kind of androgynous quality that leaves the masculinity of Christ ambiguous. Even many depictions of the Crucified Savior will present his body as so slight in build that it hardly seems a manifestation of a man whose physicality would have been conditioned by a culture that demanded physical labor for even ordinary tasks. Steinberg's thesis is not trivial, it is apt, and worthy of consideration. What has become of Christ's masculinity?

According to Steinberg, the artists of the Renaissance presented the reality of Christ's masculinity in ways that we now find disconcerting and off putting. Images of the nude Christ-child are a case in point, as many of these images came be in later times "adjusted" by painting swaddling clothes so as to make the paintings conform to the sensitivities of the later viewers. The revelation in these paintings is not God just as a baby, but God as a male child with all the attributes that come with this designation. Further, many Renaissance depictions of Christ Crucified or of his Resurrection will actually depict, through a provocative use of the garments covering the Lord's body, that the body that suffers and rises from the dead is distinctly male. This was done, because the masculinity of Christ was seen as something that while controversial, was not offensive. The body of Christ's human nature was male, and like a male, to paraphrase the *Letter to Hebrews*, in all things but sin.

How we have moved from the blatantly masculine images of Christ preferred by many artists of the Renaissance to the de-sexualized images of Christ that remain so prevalent today is an important question that deserves an answer. The emergence of feminism as an ideology cannot bear singular responsibility as images of Christ which eschew a presentation of his form as distinctly masculine predate feminism. Though it must be said that it is partly a result of the insistence that Christ's masculinity can be problematic to some that has led to the evasion of the theological significance of his decision to effect human salvation by accepting as his own a human body that is distinctly male. As an advocate of feminist theology one time said to me "It is not his masculinity that matters, but that Christ was human." I don't think that kind of dialectical thinking really works. The male body of Christ's human nature must mean something—or God would have accomplished our redemption through a different kind of body.

It isn't just the avatars of feminism that find the masculine body of Christ to be problematic. After all, many of the artistic representations of Christ that seem so androgynous are the images of popular devotion and piety. It is in regard to the masculinity of Christ that those who advocate critiques of the Faith are oddly in sync with those who present themselves to be the Faith's staunchest supporters. For both, yet for different reasons, the masculinity of Christ is a problem. What is at the root of this? Perhaps it is a kind of Gnosticism, overt in terms of feminist theology and covert in popular piety. This Gnosticism is a myth making venture where the narrative of the Incarnation is reconstructed so as to diminish the significance of Christ's masculinity to such an extent that it virtually disappears

The male body of Christ is problematic for feminists because it is male. The male body of Christ is problematic for others because the human body is almost exclusively understood as an occasion of sin and something from which the soul must be liberated in order for true spiritual attainment to be achieved.

Neither perspective resonates with a genuinely catholic and orthodox sense of the Incarnation. For the artists of the Renaissance, the densely textured humanity accepted by God in Christ was the reason for their unrestrained presentation of the masculinity of the Savior. God had, in Christ, accepted a human nature and without any compromise to his divine nature, had lived a real, human life. It was this greatest mystery of the Catholic Faith that empowered them to present the Lord as a distinctly human male. We might for the sake of ideology protest against Christ's masculinity or for the sake of modesty seek to disguise its reality, but whatever we gain from our protests, we lose in understanding.

The Incarnation does not mean that God in Christ achieves a resemblance of a human nature which he employs as a kind of ruse. Christ does not just appear to be human—he is human and this is how our own communion with his divine life is accomplished. Certainly there is a distinction. Christ does not experience our humanity as one who is fallen like us, but he does experience the effects of our fallen condition inasmuch as creation itself languishes under the influence of our sin. This fallen nature, though not his own, presses upon him with crushing intensity from the outside, represented by the crowds that gather around him and finally in the weight of the cross. Further, as the Council of Chalcedon made clear, the relationship of the divine and human natures in Christ is "without confusion or change, division or separation". In other words, divinity and humanity are not in conflict with one another in Christ, but in perfect communion. But this communion does not mean equivalence, the divine nature is greater than the human nature, even while it does not cancel out or destroy its reality.

And all of what I have described, the sheer wonder of the Incarnation, what the Fathers of Church described a "a marvelous exchange", reveals itself to the world in the God-man Christ. Yet why is Christ's apparent and very real masculinity significant? What might it engender in terms of a spirituality of vocation and of the Christian life? Saint Bernard of Clairvieux imagined the masculinity of Christ as complement to the reality of the soul that he saw as best symbolized as feminine in its receptivity to God. This mystical rapport of the feminine soul and the masculine Christ characterizes much of Catholic spirituality. It has profound resonance in the experiences of female mystics, and it is also a primary metaphor in the writings of St. John of the Cross. In my experience, many men find this imagery perplexing as it seems to necessitate a bracketing of a reality they experience as integral to their identity—even if the soul is understood as feminine in its receptivity to the overtures of divine love, their deepest sense of self is not feminine, but masculine, and their receptivity to God is understood in terms of what it means to be a man. Because so much of the Church's spiritual treasury presents the dynamism of the feminine soul meeting the masculine Christ, men, while discerning much they can appreciate, find little that they can apply to immediacy of their concerns. The presentation of so much imagery in which Christ appears androgynous furthers the experience of dissonance as men seek a spirituality that is both Christian and masculine.

While giving Saint Bernard and so many of the Church's saints and mystics the credit and deference they deserve, might there be another way to appreciate the masculinity of Christ as a spirituality of the Christian life? I think so. The presentation of Christ as being distinctly male is important as well as understanding that his masculinity is employed in the manner akin to that of a Sacrament, through which a divine gift is offered and can be received. That gift directs us to the salvific and redemptive import of the Incarnation. Christ who lived as a man, elevates masculinity in its potentiality from being simply an expression of the merely natural, to becoming a route of access to communion with God.

The *Catechism of the Catholic Church* identifies a Sacramental as a visible sign of the hidden reality of salvation. In this respect, Christ the Lord can be understood as a Sacrament, as can the Church. This understanding stretches the popular understanding of a Sacrament as being just the Seven Sacraments. My intention is not to negate the Seven Sacraments or add to their number, but to complement the reality of the Seven Sacraments with an insight concerning the deeper reality of Christ that they all signify. The Seven Sacraments are occasions or opportunities through which the faithful encounter and participate in the divine life of Christ. The Lord Jesus is the primordial ground of the ontology and action of the Seven Sacraments and he invests his power to impart his gifts through the Seven Sacraments to the Church. This is what the *Catechism* means when it so eloquently expresses the reality of the Seven Sacraments as "powers that come forth" from the Body of Christ, which is ever living and life giving. They are actions of the Holy Spirit at work in his Body, the Church. They are masterworks of God in the new and everlasting covenant."

Note the imagery employed here is not the same as the mystical language employed by the mystics which describes the feminine soul's receptivity to the masculine Christ. Instead, the language is decidedly masculine. What the artists of the Renaissance displayed about the Incarnation figuratively, the *Catechism* is expressing linguistically. The Church is Christ's Body, an extension of the Body of the Lord revealed in the Incarnation, whose life giving power manifested by the Holy Spirit, emanates from the Body of Christ and expresses itself in the Seven Sacraments. The Seven Sacraments are expressive of divine power and will, meant as effective agents of salvific transformation and are an encounter with the Incarnation that extends from the heavenly to the earthly into the Church. The Seven Sacraments introduce us and allow us to participate in the Incarnate Lord, who is himself the primordial Sacrament, and through whom the Seven Sacraments are created and made efficacious. The Seven Sacraments are an encounter with the Body of the Lord that is revealed to us in the Incarnation.

My point here is that because the Incarnation is condition for the possibility of the Seven Sacraments, that Christ has determined by his own divine power and will to be the privileged means by which humanity will encounter him and share a relationship with him, the masculinity of Christ is an unavoidable fact of our experience of the Sacraments, as it is an unavoidable fact of the Incarnation itself. The Sacraments do not introduce us to Christ as an abstraction, but we are introduced to the Christ who is revealed in the Incarnation, the God-man from Nazareth. The language of the Catechism suggest this as it associates the Seven Sacraments as expressions of divine power and will that effect a participation for the faithful in the Church as the Body of Christ, a Body for which our reference point for understanding is to be the body Christ accepted in his Incarnation. The Church is not here, at least in this description, simply a feminine receptacle which receives divine grace, but it is a revelation of the Body of the Lord himself, and the Sacraments are expressive of the power of that Body as he continues to labor and work on behalf of humanity.

The imagery here emphasizes what the Body of Christ is doing and in this respect, rather than simply identifying the passive receptivity of the soul to receive the Sacraments, the emphasis is on Incarnate Christ and what he affects. It is the work of the Incarnate Christ to make the Seven Sacraments and sustain them with his divine life. This is what the Body of Christ (the Incarnation) extended in space and time in the Church is doing right now. The Incarnation takes what is carnal and elevates it through communion with a divine nature to a participant in that divine nature. This is the logic of the Incarnation and a similar logic holds for the Seven Sacraments.

The Seven Sacraments are not only gifts that come to us from Christ, but they are also a way of life, forming, as the *Catechism* attests, "an organically, structured priestly community." Understand community here not simply as a kind of institution, but as a way of being, thinking, acting, receiving and giving. This way of life becomes, through participation in the Sacraments, a representation, to more and less degrees, of Christ himself. The spirituality or way of life that this engenders is to be like Christ and to do what he does. It is precisely with this spirituality of Christ-likeness in mind that I think that a spirituality of masculinity might find its meaning and purpose. As the Incarnation is the proper reference point for Christian spirituality, Christ's masculinity, evidenced in the Incarnation, becomes the proper reference point for what God intends for masculinity.

Christ's masculinity is represented in the Body of his Incarnation, but it cannot be reduced to the biological realities that made the body of his human nature male. The masculinity of Christ is significant, not simply because it is masculine, but because Christ elevates that masculinity through communion with his divine nature. Abstracting the significance of Christ's masculinity from the dynamism of the Incarnation makes it merely an accidental characteristic of the Incarnation, worthy perhaps of consideration for its cultural meaning, rather than a reality that is integral to the revelation of the Incarnation of the Lord. In other words, there is a divine purpose being expressed in the presentation of the Body of Christ as male. The reality of Christ's masculine body is intended to signify the manner in which God relates to his creation in Christ. I believe the Church expresses this relationship in its description of how the Seven Sacraments gain their power and efficacy from the Incarnation, but we can also consider the qualities through which Christ acts as a man as imparting to us the meaning of not only his own masculinity but also our own. These qualities through which Christ manifests his masculinity can serve as reference points for a spirituality of masculinity that can be a complement to the feminine imagery that has been favored by the Church's saints and mystics. I will highlight three qualities or actions which I think are important: Christ's suffering; Christ's sacrifice; and Christ's nuptial union with the Church.

The *Letter to the Hebrews* expresses one of the great mysteries of the Incarnation through an incredible assertion "Son though he was he learned obedience from what he suffered." Why would the divine Christ, whose human will was in perfect sync with his divine will need to learn obedience? And further how are we to understand his sufferings in this regard. A helpful way of understanding the testimony of the Letter to the Hebrews is to consider the extent to which Christ accepts the reality of a human nature. If that acceptance was merely a kind of fabrication or a conceit, Christ would have revealed himself not simply as human, but as a kind of super human, more akin to the demi-gods of mythology rather than the divine person who is described in the Gospels and professed by the Apostolic Faith. Further, by suffering, we do not have to simply understand Christ's endurance of physical pain or emotional anguish, the kind of which would have been extraordinary in his Passion and Death, but it is also signifies the reality of the human experience of limitation.

God in Christ accepts for himself the limits his human nature imposes and works within those limitations to accomplish his solidarity with our condition. I know the implications of this can be controversial, but the alternative to Christ's acceptance of the limitations of his human nature seems to me to reduce that human nature to a semblance, rather than a reality. In accord with the insights of Saint Gregory Nazianzus and St. Athanasius, one of the truths of the Incarnation is that in regards to Christ's human nature, what he did not assume or accept for himself, he cannot be said to have been redeemed. Christ must, according to an orthodox understanding of Christology affirmed by the *Letter to the*

Hebrews, be like us in all things but sin. Therefore the stakes are high. The tendency to sequester the implications of the limits Christ accepted so that his experience of a human nature would be real, rather than a fabrication, makes people cautious. However, as Saint Gregory and Saint Athanasius indicate, the stakes of reserving some of the harder facts of the human condition from Christ has profound implications.

The hardest fact for many to consider is not so much Christ suffering physical pain, but that he allowed himself to experience life as a learner like ourselves, meaning that he came to terms with life through trial and error as we do. He had to learn to crawl and to walk. He learned what it meant to be an Israelite as if for the first time. His parents would have had to help him shape sounds into words and words into sentences and then show him how written symbols could represent those spoken words in writing. He would have had to strengthen his body and perfect the requisite level of skill so that he could apply himself to his trade. In other words, he did accept a free pass in these regards, but as the magnificent *Letter to the Philippians* witnesses "he emptied himself, taking the form of a slave." This slavery should not be reduced to the sociological implications of being born in the peasant classes of a territory occupied by a foreign power, but instead slavery implies the limitations imposed on him by his acceptance of a human nature. He willed to be subject to those limitations. The Letter to the Hebrews also insists that he endured these limitations without sin, meaning that the fallen desires of concupiscence that afflict our own experience of the limits of a human nature did not influence Christ's experience of limitation.

A helpful way of understanding this might be to consider that he aspired against these limitations in the manner that an athlete perfects their performance by setting themselves against ever more difficult goals. I think this might be key to understanding Christ's suffering, his experience of limitation. His approach was comparable to athletic aspiration, to the development of skill, strength and endurance that prepares one for contest. Obedient to the purpose for which he accepts the limits of a human nature, he engages those limits in such a manner that his experience can become a source of perfection for our own human nature. In other words, not needing the benefit that accrues to himself for what he suffers for, he gives the benefit of his suffering to us.

Christ trains for the contest, triumphs through his efforts, and gives us the prize.

What might be the lesson in terms of masculinity that is displayed in the willingness of Christ to accept suffering and limitation? Primitive peoples likely understood better the necessity of men learning what was required of them through rituals of initiation that brought them face to face with suffering and limits. These culturally determined experiences of risk and danger enabled men to learn just what their natural skills of intellect, strength, and will were for—not just for their benefit or for the purpose of aggression but for the sake of purposes that transcended their own self interest. In his willingness to accept suffering and limitation, Christ indicates that his purpose is not self interested—a purpose that reveals itself in the most startling way on the cross. His acceptance of a human nature was not so that he could have something for himself, but so that he might give his life, his divine life, to us. His acceptance of the raw facts of life, including suffering and death, transforms our own experience of those realities into occasions where we can encounter God. Therefore, a masculinity that has been elevated by Christ imitates the willingness to endure limits for a purpose that transcends self-interest. Christian masculinity strives, with athletic focus, against limits so that a greater good can be accomplished and that good can be delivered to the benefit, not of the self, but of the other.

Christ's masculinity also reveals itself in sacrifice. As the theologian Father Robert Barron has noted in his reflections on the nature of the Eucharist, there is no love in this world without sacrifice. Sacrifice is the condition for the possibility for the manifestation of love, not simply a feeling, but as an act of the will to seek another person's good. Love is an act of the will in which we desire the good for another person. This act of the will endures beyond affectation and feeling, even while it can include these things, but reducing love to affectation and feeling is replace real love with a counterfeit experience.

The Gospels are from start to finish the story of a sacrifice. The drama of the Gospels is that God in Christ makes of himself the sacrifice that Israel longed to offer to God, but could not. This sacrifice was mercy, and Christ became this mercy in a concrete form. Once this form reveals himself to the world, it is clear what he is to become—an offering, which could accomplish the reconciliation of God and his people—divinity and humanity. John the Baptist's proclamation of Christ as the Lamb of God gives us the clue that unlocks the mystery of the Incarnation: God has come in Christ to be a sacrifice. This sacrifice will accomplish what no mere worldly sacrifice could.

God and humanity share communion with one another in Christ and this communion is an expression of love as it is the perfect manifestation of God willing what is the highest good for us. All worldly goods, conditioned by finitude, will pass away; but God, who is the infinite Good, is eternal and therefore superior to any other good to which we might aspire to attain. It is through Christ's sacrifice, his willingness to love us in such a way that he gives to us what we cannot attain for ourselves, that we receive an infinite Good—communion with God. The Incarnation accomplishes this through Christ's acceptance of the full implications of what it means to be human, including the realities of suffering and death. His willingness to do this, for our sake, is the sacrifice that is pleasing to the Father. God in Christ accepts a human nature, not because he needs to, or because we have earned such a privilege, but because God loves us and desires that we would have a good that we could not deserve or earn.

Further, Christ accomplishes in his acceptance of a human nature a reconciliation with us that we could not effect by own efforts. The estrangement from God that has been caused by human resistance to God's will and purposes for true human flourishing introduced into the human condition a corruption of our nature that could not be rectified by any project that was intended to perfect the human condition. Even the Law of Moses, bound so closely to culture and custom that were themselves implicated in our resistance to God's will and purposes, could not accomplish reconciliation with God and restoration of humanity's relationship with him. The means by which this restoration of humanity's relationship with God could happen had to be from God's own initiative, whose nature had not and could not be compromised by humanity's resistance. As St. Anselm so joyfully observes in this regard, God doesn't have to do anything to set right a human project that had by our own efforts gone so wrong. But God does! He intervenes in Christ, not out of obligation or because we deserve it, but out of love for us. This love is manifested in the sacrifice of the Incarnation, Christ's acceptance of the full implications of a human nature that includes suffering and death. This is the sacrificial love that reconciles us to God and offers to us communion with his divine life.

What might the sacrifice of Christ reveal about how a properly reconciled soul appropriates and understands God's will and purposes in regards to masculinity?

Christian masculinity expresses itself in a willingness to attain a good for others, even if it means that a man must make a sacrifice so that this good can be attained. If through suffering we accept what is necessary so that we might conform ourselves to God's will, it is through sacrifice that we seek to accomplish a higher good than what might serve our own interests- and we do so, not because the good we would impart is something that has been earned or deserved.

This is a critical move in the spiritual life because a natural sense of justice would approach love in terms of delivering only what benefits a relationship could return to you and nothing more. If God had approached his relationship in this way, there would never have been the Incarnation. God gets nothing from us that he doesn't already possess. The gift that is the Incarnation of God in Christ gives us something beyond what justice entails. The application of mere justice would have left us without recourse and bereft of communion with God. This is why the sacrifice of the Incarnation represents the perfection of mercy. Christian masculinity knows that the demands of mercy will always be necessary even after the demands of justice have been met. Bottom line: Christian masculinity knows how to forgive as Christ did—even if that forgiveness necessitates a sacrifice so that a greater good can be achieved- and even if that forgiveness looks an awful like the cross.

Finally, Christian masculinity should be nuptial. By this I mean that it should present itself to the world as an iconic representation of the love Christ has for the Church. This relationship is likened in the Scriptures as that of a bridegroom for his bride and this imagery is not incidental to either the mystery of the Incarnation or Christian spirituality. In fact, I think it is a non-negotiable necessity to our understanding of both. At the beginning of the essay, I offered Leo Steinberg's identification of the unsettling manner in which Renaissance artists portrayed

Christ's very real masculinity as a means to beg the question as to whether the masculinity of Christ has been so bracketed from our perceptions of what the Incarnation is all about, that not only has our imagery of Christ become distorted, but masculinity does not seem to have a clear reference point in Christian spirituality. Images of Christ that are androgynous are not only a paltry representation of the Incarnation, they also indicate an Incarnation that seems mitigated into its capacity to give life. Yet Christ does give life and the Sacraments of the Church are examples of his life giving power.

The Sacraments, expressions of Christ's creative potential that come to us through the Body of his Incarnation, also give life to the Church. On the level of mystery, this life giving potential that Christ imparts sacramentally to his Church, is to be understood as nuptial—the union of Bridegroom and Bride. This is the underlying metaphysic behind the Church's worship, in the Mass, which is likened in the Scriptures to Church as "the bride, the wife of the Lamb" (*Revelation* 21:9). It is through the nuptial imagery of the Mass that the mysterious relationship between the Incarnation and the Church is revealed.

It is important that Christian masculinity be fecund and generative, rather than unproductive and sterile. Masculinity contains within itself creative potential and this creative potential is ordained by divine purpose. In order for this purpose to be accomplished, a man must enter into a relationship that can receive this life-giving potential, bring it to fulfillment, and then bear it into the world. Christ does this for the Church through the Sacraments. In terms of ourselves, this is what is meant to happen in the Sacrament of Marriage, but it is also what is intended to happen for the man who receives the Sacrament of Holy Orders and takes his place in relation to the Church as Christ is related to his Bride.

Much more than symbolism is at stake in this nuptial imagery. In this case, the symbol is not meant simply to give rise to thought, it is meant to give rise to life. Christian masculinity is meant to be a creative force through which new life happens and existing life is protected and sustained. Bottom line this means that Christian masculinity entails becoming a father, if not through biological reproduction, then through the life giving regeneration of the Sacraments. Fatherhood is the ordinary way in which

Christian masculinity is accomplished, sustained and revealed. What kind of father does Christ reveal? That reality is discerned in relation to his suffering and his sacrifice.

In both the Sacrament of Marriage and Holy Orders the divine life of Christ gives rise to a new kind of life offers the possibility of a human nature can be elevated to share in a divine nature. What the divine Christ accomplishes for his human nature he intends to accomplish in us. Communion with the divine life of Christ is a living reality that the masculine body of his human nature, now perfected in the glory of his resurrection, fully reveals. The glorified body of Christ, which bears the wounds of his suffering and sacrifice, also bears the masculinity that indicates that the human nature he assumed was real, and not a fabrication. Christ's masculinity, a scandal to some, and strange and off-putting to others, is not incidental to his mysterious Incarnation, but it is a route of access by which we can participate in his divine life and an indication as to how God, through the Body of the Incarnate Lord, elevates the bodies of our human natures to share in the glory of his divine nature.

FINDING BALANCE IN MIND, BODY, AND SOUL

KEVIN VOST

JARED ZIMMERER

SHANE KAPLER

Man Up Your Mind!

KEVIN VOST, PSY.

"Contact with writers of genius procures us the immediate advantage of lifting us to a higher plane; by their superiority alone they confer a benefit on us even before teaching us anything. They set a tone for us; they accustom us to the air of the mountain-tops."

A.D. Sertillanges, O.P., The Intellectual Life

To what kind of air has your mind been breathing? The atmosphere of today's popular culture has become dank and fetid as never before. Head to a bookstore, flip on your radio, TV, or electronic device of your choice. Behold the world of the trivial, the petty, the incitements to lust, to envy, to easy mindless pleasures, to fascination with scandal and depravity, to overweening pride, to an abdication of responsibility, and to propaganda promoting an ever-growing sense of entitlement. And look at the effects on men and their families. Even secular psychologists are up in arms at the growing legions of "man-boys," young men, and even some not-so-young men, who, absorbed in modern technologies and in popular media and culture, waste away their hours and their lives in depersonalized virtual worlds, while failing at school, at work, and at love.

We desperately need to send out the clarion call for a renewal of Catholic manliness, but where are we to find its models and inspiration? Where is the genius, the greatness, the saintliness? Well, we're going to have to seek it out. It's going to take some sweat to man up our minds, some steep and challenging climbing to reach the peaks where true manliness still may be found, but the bulging mental muscles we'll build along the way will be well worth the exertion. That hard-earned mental brawn will help us pull up our sons and our son's sons to the summit of manliness as well. So how do we get to that mountain top?

Studious Minds Want to Know What's Worth Knowing

"Inquiring minds want to know," declares a supermarket tabloid so typical of our modern culture. Some 24 centuries before the dawn of *The National Enquirer*, Aristotle started his Metaphysics with a similar statement: "All men by their natures desire to know. An indication of this is the delight we take in our senses." So then, not only do great minds think alike, but great and small minds as well? Not exactly, for Aristotle also wrote that, "it is better to know a little about sublime things than much about mean things." St. Thomas Aquinas elaborated on this theme in his great Summa Theologica, (II-II, Qs. 166-167), by comparing and contrasting the vice of curiosity with the virtue of studiousness.

While we might think of curiosity as a good thing associated with a thirst for knowledge, the vice of curiosity derives from the word curia for care, implying such an excessive care for things of the world that it leads to neglect of the higher things of God. The vice of curiosity beckons us almost every moment of our lives today with our myriads of trivial electronic distractions. It feeds upon that "delight we take in our senses," but stays at the level of sensory titillation from "mean things," failing to rise to the level of the intellect and its capacity to ponder "sublime things."

Virtues are perfections of our human powers, and St. Thomas called the virtue that enables us to focus and reflect upon important things the virtue of studiousness. And so characteristic of the great saint, he did not draw his ideas and arguments out of thin air. He knew well the advice of the Scriptures to "study wisdom, my son, and make my heart joyful..." (Proverbs 37:11). He also drew inspiration from Church Fathers of genius like St. Augustine who wrote, "we are forbidden to be curious; and this is a great gift that temperance bestows." Note that St. Thomas too considers the avoidance of curiosity and the development of studiousness in relation to the cardinal virtue of temperance that moderates desires. The virtue of studiousness reigns in our desire to know what is harmful to us or what is not worth knowing, but it also fires up our desire to make the effort to learn about things that are truly worth knowing.

So how can we get studious? A. D. Sertillanges argued in *The Intellectual Life* that a man with the obligations of an active life could, even with two hours per day, live out the vocation of an intellectual as well, those two hours allotting sufficient time for profitable study and writing. Speaking as a guy who works for a living by day and pens a few books by night, I believe the thoughtful Dominican got his argument right! Though not every man is called to be a writer, professor, or professional "intellectual," every man is graced by God with a rational mind, an intellectual soul, and should build it and use it for the glory of God and the benefit of his neighbor. In even one-half hour per day, any man can embark on a program to build a manly mind, if he focuses his mind on important and inspiring things.

So what then are some things truly worthy of study for the modern Catholic Renaissance Man? We should, of course, set aside some time on a regular basis for study of the Scriptures (indeed that's another chapter) and of fundamental Church documents, like the *Catechism of the Catholic Church*; but what else? What other kinds of reading should we undertake in a life-long pursuit of a general self-education conducive to real intellectual growth? I'd like to suggest three broad areas of study that will capture the essence of manliness, and inspire us to attain it.

Philosophy: How to Think and Act Like a Man
Philosophy literally means "the love of wisdom," and every man should come to love philosophy. We can all profit great philosophical works that provide useful guides to living an honorable life, fulfilling our potentials as men. Great classic works of ethics, in particular, provide us with the best practical moral guidance that can be attained form God-given natural reason.

Aristotle's *Nichomachean Ethics* gives us an incredibly detailed analysis of the nature of virtue in general, many specific virtues in particular, such as the cardinal, moral virtues of fortitude, temperance, justice, and prudence, as well as the less-known "intellectual virtues" of science, understanding, and wisdom. Aristotle writes from the Greek tradition of arête, their word meaning "excellence," which became "virtus" (literally, manliness) in Latin, and virtue in English. He provides us as well with one of the world's greatest treatments of manly, "virtuous friendship." St. Thomas found *The Nichomachean Ethics* so profound that he wrote a commentary on its every single line and borrowed from it liberally in his treatment of virtue within his peerless *Summa Theologica*. Some may find it a bit dry and difficult though. If you're one of them, I can happily recommend a brand new Catholic book in way of introduction, Connor Gallagher's If *Aristotle's Kid had an iPod* (which should prove especially helpful to young Catholic dads as well.) Another fine introduction to Aristotle's works is Mortimer Adler's *Aristotle for Everybody*. (In fact, I'd recommend it to just about everybody.)

Moving right along in the classical world of natural ethics, though the Stoics are much aligned in some circles, these purported staid and unemotional, ancient kill-joys and party-poopers, I find them most worth the reading. St. Thomas knew them well and drew from them, even clarifying some apparent conflicts with the followers of Aristotle regarding misunderstood Stoic views of the "passions." When warning against passions, Stoics did not mean emotions themselves were evil, but only harmful emotional extremes that are not checked by reason, a view with which wise Aristotelians and Thomists will calmly, though gladly, nod their learned heads in agreement.

Just dip into the pages of Epictetus's *Discourses* to get a taste for some straightforward, earthy, humorous, and reverent council on bearing the sufferings and triumphs in life, and on facing the world as a man. "Who, then, is the invincible man? He whom nothing that is outside his sphere or moral purpose can dismay," says Epictetus, the lame former slave. If you'd care for calls to manly virtue with panache and literary elegance, just open up one of the Letters or Moral Essays of his contemporary Seneca, the mentor of young Nero. That unhappy emperor later abandoned Seneca's council and ordered his suicide, leading down the road to many Christian martyrs, and to Nero's own demise. You might finish the great Stoic triumvirate with a look at the ponderings of a far greater emperor, the Meditations of Marcus Aurelius. See for yourself how a man who defended the far reaches of the Roman Empire on frozen German rivers by day, consoled his spirit and cajoled himself to virtue with reflections on God's Providence by night.

The Catholic Renaissance Man must make time as well to find out how the learned medieval Doctors of the Church, St. Albert the Great and his greatest student, St. Thomas Aquinas, imbibed all the natural wisdom of the best of classical philosophy, baptized it with the even higher truths of Divine Revelation, and employed it in the service of theology. St. Thomas's Summas are not easy reads, but are well worth the effort, and thank God, there is certainly no dearth of good modern books that can introduce us to his manly wisdom and saintly character. A little-known book that inflamed my passion for St. Thomas' thought when I first came back to the Church was Gerald Vann's *The Aquinas Prescription.*

Among the most thoughtful recent expositions of his thought I have seen is Edward Feser's *Aquinas,* and I can hardly recommend enough many other fine works by A. D. Sertillanges, Reginald Garrigou-LaGrange, Etienne Gilson, Jacques Maritain, Fergus Kerr, Brian Davies, and so many others. And as for the philosophy of St. Thomas's teacher, I would not mind in the least if you used my own recent biography of *St. Albert the Great* as a humble introduction and springboard to books more sublime.

History: What a Man Should Know About the Past

That the Catholic Renaissance Man should study the history of the Catholic Church goes without saying, though I've just said it. There are countless works worth examining, from the 4th century Church History of Eusebius, the father of church history, through the historical writings of Catholic literary greats like Hilaire Belloc (e.g., Survivals and Arrivals), to moving modern summaries of church history like H. W. Crocker's *Triumph,* and the various books of Diane Moczar, just to name a few of a host of worthwhile possibilities.

Books by good Catholic historians will also challenge the standard canards of history that many of us were raised on. Even the standard names of eras like "The Dark Ages" for the Middle Ages of the 5th centuries through the 13th AD and "The Enlightenment" or "Age of Reason" for the 18th Century, cast the centuries of medieval Christendom in a bad light, (if not as a time of no light at all!) The term "Renaissance" itself for the 14th and 15th centuries was intended by non-Catholic historians to portray a time of a rebirth of the intellect when the world had begun to free itself from the stifling influences of the Catholic Church, having re-discovered the glory and wisdom of the pagan Greeks and Romans. To see how the human intellect was really fairing at the peak of the culture of Christendom, and how those Greeks and Romans had not been forgotten, I suggest James Walsh's book *The Thirteenth, Greatest of Centuries*. (As a triple doctorate holding M.D., Ph.D, and LL.D., it seems Dr. Walsh had manned up his mind.)

The new Catholic Renaissance Man would also do well to spend some of his study time on the great works of catholic history too, "small c" catholic, (i.e., universal), that is. God made the universe and we are its citizens. We need to render unto Caesar too, and it wouldn't even hurt to read a little of works of a couple of the Caesars themselves—like Julius Caesar's war chronicles of the Gallic and civil wars, and the aforementioned Meditations of Marcus Aurelius.

Much of the best thought of the ancient Romans was built upon the foundations of the classical Greeks. Herodotus, "the "father of history," and his History are still more than "mere historical curiosities" (a past-bashing phrase I detest!). A man needs to know things of war and of great manly societies of the past. Thucydides *History of the Peloponnesian War* will not disappoint. Knowledge of the classical Greeks is well worth the time and effort to build up the mind of the Catholic man – just ask Sts. Albert the Great and Thomas Aquinas! To imbibe but a bit of their noble Grecian spirit, read H.D.F. Kitto's *The Greeks*. To see what modern culture loses when the Greeks are forgotten, read Victor Davis Hanson's *Who Killed Homer?*

As Americans, we need to know our own history as well. Our Founding Fathers were great men too, pulling from those Greeks and Romans, and from their own Christian heritage, to craft this great nation founded upon great ideas of human rights and dignity endowed in us by our Creator. We need to become familiar with the *Declaration of Independence*, and the *Constitution* too, especially in our times when our most powerful leaders seem so unaware or so contemptuous of them.

And let's hark back to Fr. Sertillanges' sage advice once more. Let our study of history include the biographies of great men, of thinkers, of leaders, of saints, and yes of great and saintly women too. The ancient biographer Plutarch explicitly declared that he wrote his series of pairs of lives of ancient Greeks and Romans with the goal of instructing his readers in moral perfection. What an amazing array of inspiring lives from across the centuries and around the world we have in the stories of our great communion of saints. They can instruct us in an even higher perfection.

Literature: What a Man Should Aspire to Be

So many great classic works of fiction can also inform and inspire the new Catholic Renaissance Man. Indeed, in its oldest exemplars, Homer's *Iliad and Odyssey*, you will find great thoughts and deeds aplenty to ponder. They were like the Bible to that ancient Gentile people living many centuries before the coming of Christ. They examine the nature of man in relation to honor, war, friendship, family, hospitality, and the development of manly character. Many later great works in the Western literary tradition can prove especially effective in inspiring us to manliness when they portray for us great heroes. Seek out bold and manly authors unafraid to tackle great questions and display great heroes, writers like Victor Hugo, for example, who in his *Les Miserables*, gave us the noble Jean Valjean.

The Catholic man should know great Catholic literature as well—such as the great fictional works of Tolkien, Chesterton, Belloc, and the very Catholic-spirited C. S. Lewis or current books such as *The Emperor of North America* by John McNichol. Perhaps you're inspired by military manliness, of stories like the brave Spartans' defense of liberty portrayed on the screen in the movie entitled *300*, (and described Herodotus millennia ago)? If so, check out Nicholas Prata's book *Angels of Iron* for an inspiring account of the how the brave Knights of St. John (The Hospitallers) defended Catholic Malta from a huge Turkish fleet.

Every Catholic man should come to enjoy as well Louis deWohl's incredible collection of historical biographies of so many great saints. I can hardly recommend highly enough his biography of St. Thomas Aquinas, *The Quiet Light*. As a non-Catholic friend said, "it just makes you want to be a better person." And dads, though Thomas was a man of thought, he lived in a tumultuous time of conflict between popes and secular powers, and some of his brothers were soldiers. There is plenty of action in there to capture your sons' attention too. Among my favorites are de Wohl's novels of King David, St. Paul, St. Benedict, and St. Francis Xavier. They all make me want to be a better person (let alone a better writer.) These are also fun books that whole families can read and then discuss around the dinner table or later in the evening in the family room or living room. *Saints Alive!* by Dr. Andrew Seddon is sure to be a crowd pleaser.

Mountain Men of the Mind

So then, new Catholic Renaissance Man, when are you going to head to the mountains, not of Busch beer, but of lofty thoughts? It's up to us whether or not we, as men, will strive to love God with all our hearts, strength, souls, and minds. God has provided so many great men before us who will gladly show us how, but we must actively seek out their advice by immersing ourselves in the written legacies they've left us. We need not be afraid that their ideas are beyond us. They themselves will help pull us up toward their heights over time, if we cooperate with them in regular, diligent study. Is it worth one-half of an hour of time today, tomorrow, and every day, until we reach the ultimate summit and look upon the face of God?

Strength for the Kingdom: The New Asceticism

JARED ZIMMERER

"For what is more king-like than to find yourself ruler over your body after having surrendered your soul to God?"—St. Leo the Great

The role of a man can be defined by many different phases and aspects of his life. When seeking out the authentic reality of what it means to be a man, the realization of his purpose in life should be in the forefront of his studies. Who and what we are defines our purpose and as children of God our purpose is to know, love and serve Him. In fulfilling this purpose, the sacrificial characteristic of growing in physical willpower is indispensable. In a time and culture where fast food and sedentary lifestyles reign supreme, discipline and hard work might seem a bit odd but this must not deter a man from grasping that these traits are stepping stones on the pathway to perfection.

Men are very physical beings. We are meant to be in touch with nature and to physically work with our hands. There is a natural inclination within a man to want to know how to build, how to create and how to fix things. Due to the nature of our pencil-pushing American culture most men today are not in a position to satisfy that need on a regular basis. The popularity of television shows such as *Deadliest Catch*, *Dirty Jobs* or *How Things Are Made* signifies the want in all men to work outdoors and with their hands. I have heard it said that if you do not teach a young boy to create he will automatically be inclined to destroy. Judging from the up and coming generation I believe we have an entire group of young men willing to destroy that which they do not understand. Appropriating this understanding of healthy creation or unhealthy demolition with the physical aspect of the human being, it is quite apparent from the rise in obesity, sexual diseases and drug use that the proper education of why and how to build up the human body is sorely lacking.

The evident struggle to teach men the beauty of the body and the necessity of taking good care of it can be properly visualized through fitness and sports. The deeper meaning of the human body can be recognized by working through your weaknesses and realizing your strengths. When desiring to improve in health and overall fitness a man acquires much about himself, his Creator, and his meaning in life. The issues of chastity, temperance and the ever ignored vice, gluttony, are put in proper focus when a person appreciates his body for the gift that it is. By willful determination a man can decide that any inappropriate conduct would deter him from his final goal of having a body prepared for the mission ahead. Many stories can be found about young men living a decadent lifestyle that later found sports, bodybuilding or fitness training that later turned his life around. This is precisely because as the will is exercised to push through physical limitations a man learns two things: that he is mortal and that he is not made of glass.

Being strong and fit may not be the goal of most people today, but physical training allows for a well-rounded humanity. Dave Draper, a bodybuilding legend, found that living to grow in strength creates vast opportunities to grow in virtue. "Muscle, might and mind, what a select combination of qualities to contain in one body! Too often man possesses one characteristic exclusive of the others: He's strong, yet oversized and dull-witted; he's bright, but a physical wreck, or a sturdy fellow without an ounce of understanding. The three invaluable attributes come together like water, vapor and ice when man works for them with blood, sweat and tears. Now we have something special, a rare and exclusive blend: strength in all forms at once." – *Iron on My Mind*

The challenge that I propose to my readers is to keep yourself in physical shape and health for the mission God has blessed you with. Your body is a gift. You would not mistreat a brand new Maserati because of the worth it contains. Your body is infinitely worth more than any material possession or other substance on this Earth. You are created by a loving God and Christ redeemed that creation by donning flesh Himself. Through His example of physically fulfilling His mission we can take note that our mission could be just as physical which requires preparation. The 'New Asceticism', of which I will explain later, offers the chance to grow in holiness, all the while growing physically strong, agile and virile.

While we are blessed enough to live in a time where unprecedented opportunities exist for every person to take advantage of the health culture there still seems to be a disconnection when it comes to integrating it within the Catholic world. The Catholic Church heavily approves of sports and the fitness culture, so long as it is properly oriented towards Christ Himself. The Church has much to offer in the arena of keeping fit and healthy for a higher purpose. Viewing sports and competition as a healthy means of expressing yourself and growing in the virtues of fortitude, prudence, justice and temperance, the Church appreciates what physical activity can not only allow but enhance. The unfortunate suspicion of the fitness movement has occurred in the actual application of these values. Many today still see the body as the sensualistic problem guiding us towards concupiscence rather than recognizing that the building of the human body, through regular ascetical practices, can become a major factor to the solution.

The Platonic ideal of dualism, teaching that the soul is trapped in the human body, has caused a rift in the area of understanding the human being as a whole. However, St. Thomas Aquinas upholds that the human body and the human soul are not two separate entities but one nature, one single material substance, "it is clear that man is not a soul only, but something composed of soul and body." (*Summa Theologica* Ques. 75 Art. 4.). It is as the *Catechism of the Catholic Church* states: "The unity of soul and body is so profound that one has to consider the soul to be the "form" of the body: i.e., it is because of its spiritual soul that the body made of matter becomes a living, human body; spirit and matter, in man, are not two natures united, but rather their union forms a single nature." CCC# 365 (italics added). In building up the human body, the soul is therefore built upon as well. As the human body works to grow in health and robustness, the soul grows in the cardinal virtues I had mentioned before.

Before the fall of man, in the prelapsarian state of existence, Adam and Eve understood with perfect unity what the soul was for the body and the body for the soul. Thus, when viewing each other without clothes on there was no shame as Adam did not view Eve as a body containing a soul but rather saw her soul through and with her body. Viewing the body as a container of the soul rather than the same substance has led to certain ascetical practices which lead to punishing the body so that the soul can be free of the 'dead weight'. Old practices of flagellation, harsh and almost deadly fasting and other penitential punishments led to the damage of the human body rather than the building. This is not to downplay the necessity of voluntary suffering or the most holy saints who took part in these practices, what is meant to be demonstrated is that an ascetical lifestyle does not inevitably have to lead towards the destruction of the body. Instead, what I (and a few other noble men of which I am very thankful and blessed to know) have deemed as the 'New Asceticism' may explain how we can bring back the ways of discipline in order to build up the human body for its purpose, that being its mission.

In knowing and fulfilling your mission, each as different as the next, the physicality of man must be in accord with that mission in order to fulfill it. Discipline for the sake of the mission propounds the grace given as the whole purpose of disciplining the body through healthy eating habits and regular, vigorous exercise is to give Christ something more fit for ministry. In building the body for your mission in life you are properly orienting it towards the Divine. No matter what your God-given mission is, the body is an essential component. If you are called to be a public speaker, it is wearing on the body to do so. If you are called to feed the homeless, you must be healthy enough to withstand the physical toll. If you are called to spread the Good News of the Gospel of Christ through literature, exercise and healthy eating habits allow for the mind to gracefully allow the Holy Spirit to guide your hand.

The New Asceticism would not focus on the looks of the human body, each of us have our own natural proportions given to us by our Creator. While looking more beautiful is not the purpose of growing in health, the natural procurement of beauty through exercise suggests that our Creator is pleased with such practices. The New Asceticism focuses more on what exercise can do for the human person as a whole, in mind, body and soul. Growing towards perfection in these three areas of your life can encourage the path to holiness. Ascetical practices, indeed involving necessary pain, will lead the soul operative towards a deeper and more understood self-mastery. This discipline would then create a body which would be ready for any possible obstacle on his mission, or path towards holiness.

Many suppose that giving so much time and energy to improving the body seems irrational but using a pertinent quote from the Venerable Fulton Sheen who demonstrates that the health of the body is just as important as the health of the mind and growth of the soul. "Neglect the body, and the muscles stiffen; neglect the mind, and imbecility comes; neglect the soul, and ruin follows." (*Victory Over Vice* pg. 87) The celestial ladder towards heaven is paved by way of the cross; a life of comfort does not adhere well with the way of the passion. If you want to get smarter, you must stretch your mental capacities by reading a difficult book or learning a new philosophical or theological principle. If you want to grow in spiritual strength, the sometimes discomforting act of daily prayer and devotion is a pillar. The given energy, and sometimes inevitable pain, for the growth of muscle and health can remind us of our mortality and thus help us remember our soul and our mission.

The *Catechism* states in #2015: "There is no holiness without renunciation and spiritual battle. Spiritual progress entails the ascesis and mortification that gradually lead to living in the peace and joy of the Beatitudes." Mortification of the body points the person towards the Beatitudes which, simply defined, may be understood as guidelines of our sanctifying mission in life. The mortifying process of muscle growth and healthy living focuses the soul in a way that many other practices are unable to, especially for men. It is interesting to note, going back to the quote from the *Catechism* that after a hard lifting session, run, or any other physical activity, there is a peace which remains in the mind and heart of the participant. Being a weight lifter I can tell you from experience that not only does a person feel at peace but they are filled with more energy to face life's challenges and fulfill their roles in whatever state in life they have attained.

A large part of our mission to save souls denotes our own ability to master our own wills and to fight temptation. Self-mastery, a Catholic virtue, is the needed component for anyone struggling with specific sinful inclinations. This is not to undervalue God's grace in any way, without said grace the mission would be lost, but what is meant to be explained is that personal sacrifice, be it fatty foods or time out of your day to exercise primes the soul to fight manfully. G.C. Dilsaver stated in his fantastic book *The Three Marks of Manhood*: "Self-discipline develops a will that is both master over the mental, emotional, and physical faculties and a servant unto one's duty, ideals and faith." What better practice is there than living ascetically through proper training, exercise and diet, while focusing on growth for the sake of God's will for you? When you are the master of your own will your mission from God becomes the bulls-eye on which your heart is set.

Self-mastery in all things spiritual, physical and emotional bids us to become more Christ-like. By voluntarily picking up our daily crosses, whether it be sacrificing the after dinner ice cream or loading another plate onto the rack to struggle harder than the previous workout, our minds make the decision that the work must be done, our bodies do the actual work and our souls grow exponentially in willpower and grace. Christ took it upon Himself to carry, quite literally in the passion, the sins of humankind. Carrying that weight required a certain amount of preparation physically. It is as Fulton Sheen vividly stated that, "Heaven is a city on a hill. Hence we cannot coast into it; we have to climb." (*Victory Over Vice* pg. 88) Christ mastered physical self-discipline for 30 years before approaching His mission; the mystery of His corporal being solidified our call to bodily strength and vigor.

Through the mystery of the incarnation, God becoming man, we can properly deduce that the flesh is worth our time and effort. For God to belittle Himself by becoming man in the person of

Jesus Christ verifies that God believes His creation is not only good but, borrowing from the book of Genesis, it is very good. Through his physicality he redeemed mankind and brought salvation to fallen human nature. St. Thomas Aquinas stated that, "Man had withdrawn from spiritual things and delivered himself up wholly to material things…. Therefore divine Wisdom, who had made man, took to Himself a bodily nature and visited man immersed in the things of the body, so that by the mysteries of His bodily life He might recall man to spiritual life." (Aquinas's Shorter Summa #201) By donning flesh and living out a physical mission Christ pointed men's hearts towards the transcendental. The motivation of our exercise is to escalate the flesh above what our culture has made it to be.

Christ also provided an example for the preparation of the human body for mission. In the divine decision of St. Joseph as the foster-father of Jesus, our savior was raised in a home where physical work was a major factor in life. Joseph provided for his family by putting his body through the tough work of carpentry, Jesus was raised to do the same. In his 30 years living as a carpenter's son Jesus was prepared to become the spiritual warrior who later carried His cross and died for mankind. Providence wanted Jesus to be raised in an atmosphere of physical toil, thus promoting His growth into manhood by way of hardship. "Ignoring this (physical) part of an education can leave a man without the physical confidence earned from the toil and triumph of competition… It's a necessary step on the path to manhood to harness the confidence and self-knowledge that comes from this understanding of one's body. Whether big or small, strong or weak, young or old, a person who has learned what his body can and can't do is more likely to tackle life's conflicts with quiet confidence- and that is manly." - Frank Miniter *The Ultimate Man's Survival Guide*. As we are no longer living in a culture where most men take part in physical labor to provide, there is a requisite to continue the natural masculine proposition to grow physically strong. Exercise and proper diet are today's means to satisfy that calling.

Desiring to be a fit instrument in the hands of God entails preparation. Jesus primed His sacred body for the task he was meant to undertake. Exercise gives the mind, body and soul more vigorous energy to complete all that God asks of us. In Hans Urs Von Balthasar's *A Theological Anthropology* he explains Christ's training: "The long period of preparation has caused this fruit to ripen slowly to its full maturity. He has prayed, seen, been silent, fasted, and worked. He has loved His mission above everything and, at every stage in His life, has submitted, adapted, and assimilated Himself to it ever anew." (pg. 268) While His mission was the salvation of souls, He carried it out through His physical nature which could only come to fruition through preparing in mind, body, and soul.

The old ways of corporal punishment for the sake of growing in magnanimity is not a practice that needs resurgence. Instead there needs to be a new wave of men, fully expecting to be tested physically, preparing their bodies for the toll of the mission ahead. While many might incorrectly suppose that training is purely a prideful act, consistently going to the gym and eating right actually humbles a man. The new Catholic Renaissance Man would resemble Odysseus from Homer's *Odyssey*, with broad shoulders and shapely arms, to carry the weight of his purpose and the souls set in his charge. The 'New Asceticism' can create a male both stout in mind and soul. A man willing to lay his life on the line for those Christ has put into his life. Rather than focusing on the negative aspects of pain and hardship, the 'New Asceticism' would build the human being into something worthy of the cross.

"Nothing short of suffering, except in rare cases, makes us what we should be; gentle instead of harsh, meek instead of violent, conceding instead of arrogant, lowly instead of proud, pure-hearted instead of sensual, sensitive of sin instead of carnal. This is the especial object which is set before us, to become holy as He who has called us is holy, and to discipline and chasten ourselves in order that we may become so; and we may be quite sure, that unless we chasten ourselves, God will chasten us." -Blessed John Henry Newman

Greatness of Soul

SHANE KAPLER

We understand how we can develop our bodies through exercise and our minds through study, but how do we develop our souls, or spirits? After all, the soul is "that which is of the greatest value" in us, the part of us that most resembles God (CCC 363). Our bodily strength and powers of memory will wax and then gradually wane over the course of our lives, but our souls know no such limitations. It is the one facet of our nature that can increase in power from childhood straight through old age and death and into eternal life. (Our bodies will have to wait for the resurrection of the dead to catch up.)

In our Christian tradition a "great-souled" man is one who devotes himself whole-heartedly to great undertakings—he is magnanimous. Well, it is impossible to undertake a greater task than making Christ present to your family and the others around you, to lay down your life in the act of building them up and furthering God's kingdom on earth. And we find the strength to do this through an ever-deepening intimacy with Christ Jesus—a life of prayer. What's that? You don't feel like you're good at prayer? I will let you in on a secret: everybody feels that way! But listen, you are not a lone ranger trying to go it alone. Our Faith teaches that Jesus himself "prays in us and with us," making our prayer effective (CCC 2740).

The Good News, the Gospel, is that Jesus wants to catch all of us up into his relationship with the Father. In Baptism he filled us with his Holy Spirit so that we can begin to think with his mind (1 Cor.2:16), love with his heart (Rom.5:5), perform his actions (Jn.14:12; Eph.2:10), and even participate in his prayer (Rom.8:26-27)! You may be thinking, "I know how Jesus spoke and acted from reading the gospels, but I don't see much there about how he prayed." That is where I come in: I have done a fair amount of digging on this subject and am overjoyed to share how the

Eucharist and Catholic devotions and practices not only mirror Jesus' earthly prayer but join us to it. I bet you will be surprised at the richness of the words and actions familiar to Catholics the world over and how, when used intentionally, they open our souls to deeper union with Christ and, through him, the Father. Prayer is the key to becoming the great-souled men, the images of Christ, the Blessed Trinity intends.

The Foundation

Like you and me, as a man, Jesus learned to pray. That is not watered-down, "low-Christology," modernist theology talking; that is the Catechism! Yes he had a divine nature, and yes in the heights of his human soul he saw the Father as clearly as the angels in heaven; but Jesus had to learn to express his love for the Father in human words and actions, and that he learned from others. "The Son of God . . . learned to pray in his human heart. He learn[ed] to pray from his mother... in the words and rhythms of ... his people" (CCC 2599).

Jesus' prayer was Jewish prayer, and that means that the liturgy in Jerusalem's Temple was central to it. It is impossible to underestimate the Temple's value for Jews; it was holy ground, heaven's embassy on earth. Its innermost chamber, the Holy of Holies, was God's earthly throne room. Jesus called it his Father's House! Jews were required to come in pilgrimage three times a year to celebrate the feasts of Tabernacles, Passover, and Pentecost.

The worship of the Temple was built around *avodah*, sacrifice. It was the way God specifically told the Israelites he wanted to be worshiped. In sacrificing animals from their flocks and produce from their harvests, the Israelites symbolically offered themselves to God. Oftentimes part of the sacrifice was offered to God in fire upon the altar and another portion held back for the celebration of a sacred meal—God and his people were united in the life of a sacrificial victim.

There was a liturgical calendar with special celebrations and sacrifices for holy days, but I want to focus upon the Tamid, the perpetual or daily offering. Every day at 9 a.m. and again at 3 p.m.

the priests led the people in singing one of the psalms as a cake of bread, chalice of wine, and lamb were prepared for offering. As they were placed upon the enormous altar of sacrifice, a trumpet sounded and everyone in the Temple prostrated themselves to the ground in worship. One priest then entered the Holy Place, passed the twelve loaves of bread, the "bread of the Face" always kept in God's presence, and offered incense on the altar before the Holy of Holies. This was the way God had asked to be worshiped, the absolute heart of the Jewish spiritual life – just as the liturgy of the Mass is for us!

Every Sunday, we Catholics make pilgrimage to God's house to join ourselves to Jesus' sacrifice. God is present in our tabernacles in an even deeper way than in the Temple's Holy of Holies. The Tamid, the "perpetual offering," is raised to a new level as Jesus, the Lamb of God, is made present under the appearance of bread and wine. And when we receive him in communion he unites us to his Father in heaven. "Through him and with him, and in him … in the unity of the Holy Spirit," we offer ourselves and all our thanksgiving, praise, and petitions –to the Father. We Christians have come up with such a variety of ways to pray over the past two thousand years, and we can and should avail ourselves of them; but there is only one that Jesus specifically asked for, and therefore only one that absolutely none of us can omit: "This is my body … this is my blood. Do this in remembrance of me."

Building Upon the Foundation

The Lord realizes that most of us are not able to attend Mass during the work week. He has entrusted us with responsibilities— getting kids ready and off to school and/or ourselves to an early job—that simply does not make it possible. We know the power of the liturgy but cannot be in attendance, so what are we to do? Jesus, Mary, Joseph, and the millions of other Jews who lived far from Jerusalem were in exactly the same boat. Instead of throwing up their hands, they found a way to spiritually unite themselves with the offering occurring in the Temple.

Mary and Joseph taught Jesus the tradition that, at that point, their people had kept for over two hundred years. Three times a day the Holy Family, like all Jews, stopped to turn toward the Temple and pray—at 9 a.m. and 3 p.m. when the Tamid was offered, and again around sunset when the final scraps were burned on the altar and the Temple closed for the night. At the first and third times of prayer, as the spiritual bookends of the day, they recited the Shema, Judaism's Creed, composed of three passages of Scripture (Deut.6:4-9, Deut.11:13-21, and Num.15:37-41). When Jesus was asked which was "the greatest commandment," he quoted its first verses, ""Hear, O Israel: The LORD our God is one LORD; You shall love the LORD your God with all your heart, and with all your soul, and with all your strength" (Deut.6:4-5).

Like Jesus, we Christians begin and end our days, as well as our Eucharist, with a simple prayer and confession of faith: the Sign of the Cross. The Sign of the Cross encapsulates the great truths of the longer Nicene and Apostles' Creeds recited at Mass: Through Jesus' sacrifice upon the Cross we enter into the life of the Father, Son, and Holy Spirit; and by grace we are empowered to do so with all our mind (we touch our foreheads), all our heart (chest), and all our strength (both shoulders). That is our Shema, and every time we make it we petition the Lord for the grace to live it out: the very grace called down in the celebration of the Eucharist!

For Jewish men the Shema was also a daily reminder of the need to "suit up." Its final portion was the command to wear tzitzit, or tassels, at the end of their garments, "so you remember all the commands of the LORD, that you may obey them and not prostitute yourselves by going after the lusts of your own hearts and eyes" (Num.15:39). Jesus and Joseph wore tzitzit throughout their lives (Mt.9:20, 14:36). Catholics imitate them when we wear crosses, scapulars, and medals. When we glimpse them in the mirror or they feel a little scratchy, the Lord and his saints are brought to mind, and we are reminded to pray.

The Shema formed the spiritual "bookends" of a Jewish layman's day, but all three times of prayer included the Eighteen

Benedictions. They were known as Tephilla, simply "the prayer." The Eighteen Benedictions are a beautiful tapestry of blessings and petitions. I will quote just a few:

> *Blessed be the Lord, the God of Abraham, Isaac, and Jacob – our shield …*
> *Blessed be the Lord Who raises the dead …*
> *Blessed be the Lord Who loves repentance. Make us turn back to you.*
> *Blessed be the Lord Who forgives, forgive us our sins …*
> *Blessed be the Lord Who rebuilt Jerusalem. Restore the kingdom of David, your anointed*

The early Church kept the Jewish practice of blessing and petitioning God three times a day, but in place of the Eighteen Benedictions, they prayed the same prayer that was central to their celebration of the Eucharist, the Our Father (CCC 2767). Within its seven brief petitions Jesus encapsulated the whole Tephilla! In it "the only Son gives us the words the Father gave him … [Jesus] knows in his human heart the needs of his human brothers and sisters and reveals them to us: he is the model of our prayer" (CCC 2765). St. Paul wrote that it is the Holy Spirit who moves us to cry "Father!" (Gal.4:6), and the petitions that follow are those of Christ's Sacred Heart! We can pray its words exactly as they have come to us as well as a template for offering your own petition, thanksgiving, and praise. "Our Father Who art in heaven, hallowed be thy name," for example, could be followed with thanksgiving for the specific ways God has taken care of you and your family that day.

The Gospels show us how Jesus' prayer extended far beyond the day's three fixed times. He sometimes spent entire nights in conversation with the Father. In a related way, his sacrifice was not limited to the Cross, but began the very instant he was conceived (Heb.10:5-7). Jesus' every thought, word, and deed had been offered to the Father in the power of the Holy Spirit – from the obedience he gave Mary and Joseph and the work he did as a carpenter in Nazareth to his baptism (Mt.3:15), teaching (Lk.4:14-15), exorcisms (Mt.12:28), and healings (Lk.5:17).

As members of Christ's Body, we want our celebration of the Eucharist to be the culmination of an entire week offered to the Father. St. Paul told the Romans "present your bodies as a living sacrifice, holy and acceptable to God, which is your spiritual worship" (Rom.12:1). We want our every thought, word, and deed to have been offered to the Father in union with Jesus, for the Holy Spirit to unite our entire lives (serving family and friends, doing our job to the best of our ability) to Jesus' Passover to the Father. Many Catholics do this by making a "morning offering." I am fond of the offering composed by the Apostleship of Prayer:

O Jesus, through the Immaculate Heart of Mary, I offer You my prayers, works, joys, and sufferings of this day in union with the Holy Sacrifice of the Mass throughout the world. I offer them for all the intentions of Your Sacred Heart: the salvation of souls, reparation for sin, and the reunion of all Christians. I offer them for the intentions of our bishops and of all Apostles of Prayer, and in particular for those recommended by our Holy Father this month.

In its essence, true greatness of soul, or magnanimity, does not consist in undertaking projects others are able to see and appreciate, but in making an entire gift of ourselves—in each small thing we do—to God, and to others for love of God. "For this reason the Father loves me, because I lay down my life …" (Jn.10:17). "If anyone would be first, he must be last of all and servant of all" (Mk.9:35). Changing diapers, getting up and going to work day after day, keeping your temper in check, generously helping family and neighbors – that is God's idea of a great-souled man. Easier said than done, right? Don't worry; Jesus has given you his most faithful disciple as your teacher, prayer partner, and … mother.

We Need "The" Woman's Touch

You probably noticed how the morning offering above was offered to Jesus "through the Immaculate Heart of Mary." We Catholics are convinced that every man recreated in the New Adam, Jesus, is meant to share his life with the New Eve, Mary. Each of us is united to one another in the great Mystical Body of Christ. As the mother of our Head (Jesus), Mary has a special connection to each member of the Body. If we ask the Holy Spirit, he will knit our hearts together with hers, allowing us to share in the graces that adorned her soul – her prayerful union with Christ and unwavering commitment to God's will.[1]

Catholics have long recognized how Jesus gave her to us at the Cross in the person of John, the beloved disciple. Looking down, Jesus said, "Behold, your mother!" Scripture then says, "And from that hour the disciple took her into his own home" (Jn.19:27). Wherever John was, there was the Blessed Mother. I do not think it is coincidental that his is considered the most "spiritual" of the gospels with its unique focus on his divinity and his fulfillment of Israel's sacrificial worship.

It was John who gave us the Bread of Life discourse and Jesus' high priestly prayer at the Last Supper. I have to think that sharing his life with Mary had something to do with that! For nine months Jesus' Sacred Heart had physically beat beneath her own, and the flesh and blood he offered upon the Cross were taken from her. The woman who taught Jesus to pray and prayed with him multiple times a day for three decades, started praying with John. She became his mother, not just in title, but as a spiritual reality. Jesus wants that for us too.

Do you remember how the apostles prepared for Pentecost, that moment when the Holy Spirit empowered them to live and proclaim the Gospel? Jesus sent them back to the Upper Room and for nine days they "devoted themselves to prayer, together with the women and Mary the mother of Jesus, and with his brethren" (Acts 1:14). What was their prayer like? Petition, combined with a great deal of meditation—thinking and rethinking Jesus' life in the light of Scripture (see Acts 1:15-16, 2:22-36). Meditating on the life of Jesus … in the light of Scripture … in the company of the Blessed Mother—that's Rosary!

Like the Mass, the Rosary weaves together so many of the elements present in Jesus' prayer:

➢ *Sign of the Cross (Shema)*
➢ *Apostles' Creed (Shema)*
➢ *Our Father (Taught by Jesus, the encapsulation of the Eighteen Benedictions, Mt.6:9-13)*

---

[1] As a Scriptural precedent, consider 1 Cor.12:26 and 2 Kings 2:9, in light of one another.

➤ *Hail Mary (the words of Lk.1:28, 42)*
➤ *Glory Be (the words of Lk.2:14, Mt.28:19, Rev.1:8)*

Note how our lips move in the inspired words of Scripture as our hearts and minds join Mary's in meditation upon her Son's saving work. Pope John Paul II taught, "With the Rosary, the Christian people sits at the school of Mary and is led to contemplate the beauty on the face of Christ and to experience the depths of his love" (Rosarium Virginis Mariae, 1). Honestly, if Mary was deemed worthy of teaching the child Jesus to pray, and deemed worthy to help the infant Church pray its way to Pentecost, then she is certainly good enough for you and me!

Drafting Your Own Blueprint

As Catholics we have an amazingly diverse treasury of devotions the Holy Spirit has used to deepen participation in Jesus' prayer and relationship with the Father. In this brief space I have tried to show some of the powerful, and yet easy to practice, ways for growing in prayer. The most important thing is to get started. Participation in the Sunday Eucharist is an absolute, but I want to challenge you to go further and schedule three daily times of prayer. "We cannot pray 'at all times' if we do not pray at specific times, consciously willing it" (CCC 2697). How exactly you pray during those three times is of course up to you, but I obviously recommend frequent recourse to the Our Father as well as making a morning offering. To give you some ideas, I will share the pattern I have settled into:

Morning
➤ *Getting out of bed: Sign of the Cross*
➤ *In shower: Our Father and ask Mary and Joseph to intercede for various needs*
➤ *Put scapular back on (Brown Scapular of Our Lady of Mt. Carmel) and pray, "Jesus, please clothe me and my family in your Mother's prayers for our salvation."*
➤ *Taking kids to school: Spontaneous thanks and intercessions. Morning Offering*
➤ *Drive to work: Rosary*

Afternoon First 5 minutes of drive home spent using Rosary beads to pray Chaplet of Divine Mercy, which consists of:

➢ *Our Father*
➢ *Hail Mary*
➢ *Apostles' Creed*
➢ On Rosary's large beads, "*Eternal Father, I offer you the Body and Blood, Soul and Divinity of your dearly beloved Son, our Lord Jesus Christ, in atonement for our sins and those of the whole world.*"
➢ On small beads, "*For the sake of his sorrowful Passion have mercy on us and on the whole world.*"

Bedtime Grab my Bible as I climb into bed and spend 5-10 min. reading:
➢ *Usually the gospels – listening to Jesus and studying his example*
➢ *Feeds my next day's Rosary meditation, and the Holy Spirit bring verses back to me as situations arise in the course of the day*

What I am excited to share is how keeping these scheduled times of prayer has led to a lot more spontaneous prayer throughout the day (and even when I wake in the middle of the night)—and not just asking God for favors, but giving him thanks and praise! And believe me, if it has happened to me; then it can most definitely happen for you.

As I said, the key is to just get started. Grab a pencil and paper and ask the Holy Spirit to guide you in drafting your own prayer regimen. Make it realistic; look at the week ahead and schedule times and manners of prayer you know you will be able to keep. Those times will grow, of themselves. Prayer is the nurturing of a relationship and as with all relationships, conversations lengthen as intimacy deepens. The deeper we love, the more generous we are in giving of our time and energy, and the greater our souls become. But it all stems from prayer, contact with Greatness himself.

For additional information on grounding your prayer in the human prayer of Christ, please see Shane's *Through, With, and In Him: The Prayer Life of Jesus and How to Make It Our Own*

AUTHENTIC ROLES OF A MAN

DOUGLAS BUSHMAN

KEVIN LOWRY

JARED ZIMMERER

GERARD-MARIE ANTHONY

Manhood Fulfilled in Being Prolife: the Vocation of Husband and Father

DOUGLAS G. BUSHMAN, S.T.L.

The fundamental vocation and fulfillment of every man and woman is to be prolife. The reason is that every human being is made in God's image, and God is prolife. The Christian states in life and every personal vocation—marriage, ordained ministry, consecrated life, single life, and every profession, occupation and apostolate—are specifications of the universal vocation to be prolife. Thus, to be prolife is the fulfillment of manhood. Every man is called to place all of his plans and energies at the service of human life.

In union with the vocation of wife and mother, that of husband and father constitutes the primary and all-inclusive realization of the prolife vocation. Every other realization of the prolife vocation presupposes life, while the vocation of husband and father, which is always inseparable from that of wife and mother, is ordered to the generation of life and the full development of life. Teachers serve life in its intellectual and moral dimension through education, health care professionals serve life by promoting physical well-being, and clergy serve life by mediating Christ's saving truth and grace. Only spouses are entrusted with the mission to generate life and to foster its integral development, that is, its maturation in every dimension.

It is impossible to exaggerate the dignity and importance of the prolife vocation of father and husband, particularly in a culture that is anti-life. An anti-life culture is necessarily one that is anti-love and anti-God, and thereby anti-man. Put another way, an anti-life culture is built on a set of lies about what it means to be a man. It promotes a vision of manhood that is cut off from the mission to serve life and divorced from marriage. Nothing is more urgent to remedy this than a rehabilitation of the truth that manhood is fulfilled in the prolife vocation and a restoration of the dignity of the prolife vocation of husband and father.

Participation in God's Own Prolife Mission

Everything we know about what God has done in creation and salvation history revolves around His commitment to life. We could say that God assigns Himself a prolife mission. First, He creates life, fashioning man and woman in His image and likeness. Then, He imparts to them a participation in His own power to create life and blesses them with the mandate to be fruitful and to multiply (Gen 1:28). Throughout history, whenever this mandate is threatened, He intervenes to assure that it is fulfilled (Gen 8:17: 9:1, 7; 35:11; Jer 23:3; Ez 36:11). God shares His self-assigned prolife mission with His people.

God's prolife commitment comes to its summit in Jesus Christ, the Good Shepherd, who gives His life to save the lives of His sheep. He sums up His mission saying: "I came so that they might have life and have it more abundantly" (Jn 10:10). In Christ we share in God's own nature (2 Pet 1:4). We can say "I live, no longer I, but Christ lives in me" (Gal 2:20). In Christ, every Christian is consecrated to a prolife vocation. To believe in Christ and to be baptized into Him is to participate in the mission of the One Who calls Himself "the Life" (Jn 14:6).

The drama between life and death is the essential drama of human history. The Second Vatican Council (1962-65) recognized this, and renewed the Church's commitment to the divine mission to be at the service of human life and dignity. Thirty years later (1995), Pope John Paul issued his encyclical, The Gospel of Life, to proclaim God's own joy over life and the Church's mission to participate in this divine joy while engaging in every activity to serve, to protect, and to promote the fullness of life that God intends for all.

The Prolife Vocation, Holiness, and Love

God's prolife mission is rooted in His very being. It has no other explanation than His eternal perfection, that is, His holiness, "the inaccessible center of his eternal mystery" (CCC, 2809). God does not cling to this holiness as private property; rather, He desires to share it: "Be holy, for I am holy" (Lev 11:44; 1 Pt 1:16). The Second Vatican Council made this the heart of its teaching: "everyone ... is called to holiness ... and to the perfection of charity." "Charity is the soul of holiness" (CCC, 826).

Here we arrive at the essence of the prolife vocation. It is universal because it is identical with the call to perfect charity. Everyone is called to love as Christ has loved us (Jn 13:34). To be a husband and father is a particular way to live out the call to holiness and the call to be perfect in charity.

To love is to desire the fullest happiness for those one loves, and to do whatever one can do to make this full happiness a reality. It means to exert oneself to provide every good thing needed for that abundant life that is God's gift in Christ. To love as God loves us is to desire the goods that God desires, according to His set of priorities. There are many goods that we can desire: physical, intellectual, and spiritual. The highest good is God Himself. While husbands and fathers have the responsibility to provide for all the needs of those they love, there is only one good that lasts for eternity. The prolife vocation of husbands and fathers is fulfilled by a love that knows how to prioritize, believing that by seeking first God's kingdom, all other goods will follow (Matt 6:33).

We can now assert that a man who responds to the call to holiness as a husband and father defines his life in terms of a love that is free, total, exclusive, fruitful, and faithful. He commits himself to strive for the perfection of charity with his wife, to a mutually self-giving love according to God's hierarchy of goods. As a young man put it when seeking permission to marry a man's daughter: "I pray that you will entrust me with the privilege of helping her on the path to holiness and heaven, and I hope that you will bless me with the gift of her help in my own journey. I love her, I desire her true good."

The Perfection of Love

A man fulfills the vocation of husband and father when he is free from self-centeredness to fill his days with the preoccupation:

What is the most loving thing? How do I best love my wife and my children? It is a great grace to be freed from selfishness so as to ask these questions. It is an even greater grace to put the answer into practice. This is that supernatural freedom that comes with the gift of the Holy Spirit. It is freedom to serve: "For you were called for freedom, brothers. But do not use this freedom as an opportunity for the flesh; rather, serve one another through love" (Gal 5:13). The vocation of husband and father channels this freedom toward the prolife mission by serving wife and children.

To reach the heights of this service-oriented love requires that a husband and father embrace the evangelical counsels of poverty, chastity, and obedience. This will sound strange to those who think that these are restricted to religious. But, if we attend to the inner dynamism of these counsels, we discover that they are indispensable for the perfect freedom that is the condition of perfect love.

Each counsel removes an impediment to perfect love. We know that things, possessions, often become the occasion for disputes and tension in relationships. The spirit of poverty assures that a man does not inordinately value his possessions so that his relationships are not sacrificed for the sake of wealth or some cherished object. Chastity concerns a mature self-control without which true love is impossible. Without chastity a relationship can be reduced to one in which a woman's value becomes a function of her ability to fulfill a man's primal desire. By extension, it brings order to all passions, such as anger and the pleasures that accompany eating, drinking, and relaxing. Again, the primacy goes to relationships. Perfect love requires that a husband and father be able to control his desire for pleasure for the sake of those relationships. Obedience to God, to the Church, and to all legitimate authority safeguards against the imposition of a man's will in his relationships. Obedience to these authorities is the best guarantee that any use of paternal authority will be a service to life rather than crass willfulness, domination, or utility.

The greatest freedom is that which accompanies perfect love. We all know moments when our love for others is so great that it takes over, overpowering all other desires, taking us outside ourselves as if we existed only for the sake of enriching the lives of those we love. This is the experience of the liberating power of love. At such moments no possession, passion, or desire to impose one's own ways can interfere. At such moments who a man is and what he does are fused. These are moments when the prolife vocation and manhood are fully achieved.

Humility: the Foundation for Fulfilling Manhood as Husband and Father

Manhood comes to perfection for a husband and father when he fulfills his vocation by rising to the demands of love of God, love of wife, and love of children. The man who aspires to this will need to be aware of his weaknesses, become humble, and commit himself to a program of spiritual growth and conversion.

The vocation to the perfection of love as husband and father is beyond the reach of any man. Perfect charity can only be attained through the graces of the sacraments of Baptism, Confirmation, Marriage, Confession, and the Eucharist. It is not received as an object that becomes a man's possession that he can carry around with him the way he owns his clothes or his computer. A wedding is not a transaction in which the vocation becomes a man's property. It is the beginning of a new prolife partnership with God and his wife, a partnership that begins with Baptism, is strengthened in Confirmation, and fortified in the Eucharist. God is the senior partner, and the junior partner cannot hope to make his unique contribution independently of Him. The most fundamental exigency of the prolife vocation of husband and father is to remain in profound communion with the Lord: "I am the vine, you are the branches. Whoever remains in me and I in him will bear much fruit, because without me you can do nothing" (Jn 15:5).

If God had not taken the initiative and called men to be husbands and fathers, who would dare to take it upon himself? Who is advanced enough to love his wife so perfectly as to be a witness to Christ's love for the Church? Who is sufficiently virtuous and self-controlled always to do what is best for his children? If, when contemplating the exalted dignity of the Sacrament of Holy Orders, men feel "an urgent call to conversion" (CCC, 1589), those who consider the exigencies of perfect love in marriage should also have a sense of the need for conversion in order to measure up to the greatness of the vocation of husband and father.

Humility, then, is the essential foundation for the fulfillment of manhood in the vocation of husband and father. The One Who calls is faithful. God provides the grace men need to measure up to the call: "for nothing will be impossible with God" (Lk 1:37); "for God all things are possible" (Matt 19:26). Man's part is to acknowledge his dependence on the Lord and to ask Him for the grace he needs to fulfill the mission that God entrusts to him. "God resists the proud, but gives grace to the humble" (James 4:6). The best way for a man to love his wife and children is to let God love him.

The fulfillment of manhood in the vocation of husband and father, then, requires that a man make himself available to the sources of grace. These include the sacraments, daily prayer, reading Scripture, study of the Catechism of the Catholic Church, and annual or semi-annual retreats. When possible, these should be coordinated with his wife, with whom he has become one. In addition, many men are finding that men's conferences, prayer groups, and discussion groups are also sources of the grace they need to fulfill their vocation.

To be a Man, to be Male, is to be Defined Relationally

The obvious cannot be taken for granted. The proper way to understand God's plan for men is to think in terms of relationships. This is because the being of God—Father, Son, and Holy Spirit—is relational, and we are made in His image. For husbands and fathers this means that a man's identity is determined by his relationships with God, his wife, and his children.

To define oneself relationally means that relationships are the measure of happiness and success in life. It means that these relationships have more value than what one accomplishes at work. We could put it this way: how one lives in terms of the relationships with God, wife, and children, is more important than what one achieves through work. St. Joseph is the unsurpassed model of what this means. Everything we know about him boils down to his relationships with God and with Mary and Jesus.

In relation to God, Joseph is a just man (Matt 1:19). This means that he is ever ready to perform whatever God's law requires of him. We see this when Joseph and Mary go to the Temple to fulfill what the law of Moses prescribes (Lk 2:22-24, 27), and in the Holy Family's annual pilgrimage to Jerusalem for the Passover (Lk 2:41). God blesses Mary and Jesus through Joseph when he faithfully follows heaven's directive to take the Holy Family to Egypt in order to avoid the barbarous edict of Herod (Matt 2:13-19). Joseph conforms his life to the Lord's decrees, and he does this with Mary and Jesus and for Mary and Jesus. They are all one in loving obedience to the Lord. And it is significant that Jesus' first appearance in the Temple, in His Father's house, is due to Joseph's fidelity to the divine commands. God works through Joseph's obedience. Through him Mary and Jesus are blessed.

Joseph fulfills his vocation as husband and father by putting God first. In this way he serves Mary and Jesus, doing what is best for them. It could not be otherwise, since the One who called him to be husband and father also loves Mary and Jesus. In God's plan, Joseph has the exalted role of being God's associate in this love. Putting God first as Joseph did is the condition for a man to love his wife and children, and for God to love his wife and children through him. This entails several things, only a few of which can be mentioned here.

Observing the Lord's Day

"The Sabbath was made for man ..." (Mk 2:27). A man's family is part of the larger family of God, and God's family comes together on Sunday to celebrate the saving love of Christ our Lord. The weekly rhythm of rest from quotidian occupations liberates a family for worship, strengthening relationships, and serving those who are less fortunate. An anti-life culture usurps the Day of the Lord, turning it into a Godless string of activities. The prolife vocation of fathers and husbands safeguards it as a precious gift to get in touch with the Source of all life.

Daily prayer

One of the most valuable gifts a husband and father can give to his wife and children is the habit of daily prayer. A husband and father who puts God first shares his life of prayer with his family. His prayer becomes one with his wife's prayer, and together they bear witness to the heart-to-heart dialogue with God to their children. A man of faith participates in Christ's own zeal for His Father's house (Jn 2:16-17) and work, with his wife, to make his own home copy or extension of God's house, a place where people are aware of God's presence. A Catholic home should be a house dedicated to that spiritual worship (Rom 12:1) that includes daily prayer. Religious art – pictures of the Holy Father, icons, statues of Mary and other saints – can contribute greatly to creating a prolife environment that is conducive to prayer and to the practice of all the Christian virtues.

Confession

The man who puts God first is a man of conscience. He knows the high standard to which he is called, and he cannot remain deaf to the voice of conscience when it witnesses to sin. He will exemplify the humility of ongoing conversion, and by going to Confession with his family, he will bear witness to the limitless mercy of God. Weakness and sin do not have the last work, God's reconciling mercy does. He will live the graces of Confession in his family life, readily forgiving any offenses against him and, just as importantly, asking forgiveness from his wife and children. He will take the patience and forgiveness of the father of the prodigal son as his standard, and make his home a place of reconciliation.

Service

Service is active love. It is the exercise of one's gifts for the betterment of others. The family is a school of this active love of service. This entails the internal service of family members to one another, and the external service of the family as whole to others outside the family, especially the poor and suffering. Children learn and prepare for their own vocations in the prolife mission of the Church from their parents.

The Primacy of Conscience

The most effective way for a man to fulfill his prolife vocation as husband and father is by being a man of conscience. By heeding the voice of conscience, a man puts God first in all things, like St. Joseph, and this is what is best for his wife and children. In his conscience, "man detects a law ... written by God", a "law that is fulfilled by love of God and neighbor" (Vatican II). By acting in keeping with God's law known in his conscience, a husband and father makes God Himself present in the family. Very importantly, this assures his wife and children that his paternal authority is not absolute. It is subordinate to God. It is a service to the life of his family.

Being a man of conscience brings the mission of John the Baptist to fulfillment, namely, to "turn the hearts of fathers to their children" (Lk 1:17). A man of conscience is consumed with his prolife mission and defines himself in terms of service to the unity and holiness of his wife and children. This is a joint mission that a man fulfills in cooperation with his wife. The goal of this mission is to raise children to be men and women of conscience. This is accomplished through an educational process that is unique to the family. Together with his wife, a father transmits a tradition of truths, values, and virtues, all rooted in God's law known by conscience.

Cardinal Ratzinger once remarked that Christ governs the Church through consciences. It stands to reason, then, that He should govern the domestic Church, the family, in the same manner. In imitation of Christ, the proper exercise of paternal authority must always be directed to the formation of children's consciences. This means that a husband and father must live in conformity with the truth, and this will assure that his actions fulfill the prolife mission that he exercises jointly with his wife. To seek the truth, to acknowledge the truth, and to conform his thoughts, words, and deeds to the truth—this is the supreme fulfillment of manhood. This assures that every thought, word, and deed will enrich his own life and the lives of those around him. To do this in union with his wife and to raise his children to do the same is the supreme fulfillment of the vocation of husband and father, the supreme service to the life of the soul.

This primacy of conscience, and with it truth and love, reflects the way the Bible speaks about the gift of redemption in Christ. He died in order to purify our consciences by His blood (Heb 9:14). Baptism into Christ is the attestation of a pure conscience (1 Pet 3:21). By asking the Church to baptize the children entrusted to him and his wife, a man pledges himself to work tirelessly to safeguard and to educate his children's pure conscience. He does this by witnessing to the primacy of truth in conscience and by ordering family life, in his joint mission with his wife, so that his children's consciences develop properly.

Moments of conscience are the most human of all moments; they are the very essence of that abundant life that is Christ's gift to us. The prolife vocation of a husband and father is that his children become men and women of conscience, self-moving persons who have internalized God's truth. There is nothing more important in the prolife mission of a father than to be an example for his children and to reinforce them when they seek the truth, acknowledge the truth, and conform to the truth. This deserves higher praise than accomplishments in sports. A man's greatest gift to his children is a conscience that is always alert to the demands of the truth. Of course, this is not his gift to give. It is Christ's gift. And this is why the foundation of a father's prolife partnership with Christ is to present his children to the Church for Baptism, and then to preserve, defend, and develop that gift throughout his children's lives. This is a true spiritual paternity, the complement in his prolife mission to procreate.

Keeping Work in Perspective
In terms of hours per day, work comprises the majority of the vocation of husband and father. Here again, St. Joseph is our

model. Though his workdays are not described in detail, Scripture makes it clear that he was a carpenter. The fact that Scripture says more about his relation to Mary and to Jesus is significant. His craft as a carpenter was secondary. It was ordered to his relationships with God and Mary and Jesus. By his work Joseph provided for the Holy Family. This was his first and highest motive. At the same time, he provided a valuable service for those around him.

Certainly, Joseph worked as a carpenter before his betrothal to Mary. Work has an intrinsic dignity that does not depend on whether a man is married. But, for those who are husbands and fathers, work is invested with all the love that they have for their wives and children. They work because God commanded it and so as to provide for the essential needs of those they love.

Realizing this, husbands and fathers need to make decisions regarding work in light of their principal, prolife vocation of love. Is this form of work good for my family? Will this promotion deepen my relationships with God, wife, and children, or will it diminish them? The fulfillment of manhood in being a husband and a father requires that men think in terms of the primacy of these relationships. For a man to put his career first is tantamount to saying that his primary vocation is to excel to the maximum in his job. It is a most lamentable state of affairs when men work hard to super-provide for the physical goods of their families while neglecting the one thing that only a husband and father can give, namely, paternal love. Some men literally work themselves to death to provide insurance policies to protect their families from financial hardship related to death or catastrophic health care needs, only to deprive them of that interpersonal and spiritual dimension of the prolife vocation. Certainly the importance of work and a stable income is such that accommodations have to be made to the demands of a job. Yet, to the extent possible, work should be kept in the perspective that is consistent with the prolife mission entrusted to husbands and fathers. This will include the discipline of assuring that the Lord's Day retains its purpose of being a time especially dedicated to the prolife vocation by worshipping the Source of life, and by deepening family ties through worship, recreation, and service to the poor.

Concluding Remarks

The rehabilitation of the truth that manhood is fulfilled in the prolife vocation and a restoration of the dignity of the prolife vocation of husband and father are vital elements of the New Evangelization. The necessary starting point is the witness of those men who by God's grace have been blessed to know the truth about themselves and to embrace their vocation as husband and father. The urgent need is for these men to support one another and to remain attached to the Vine, without Whom they cannot remain faithful to their vocation. The world is in desperate need of the witness of joy that comes with living an intensely meaningful life. Men who live the vocation of husband and father need to demonstrate that with their prolife vocation comes a higher happiness than anything the anti-life culture can offer. Configured to Christ the King, for Whom to rule is to serve, they need to see themselves as the front line soldiers in the battle for what it means to be a man. Their vocation and spirituality is that of the Lord Himself: "No one has greater love than this, to lay down one's life for one's friends" (Jn 15:13). To lay their lives down for their wives and children so that they may have the abundant life for which Christ died, this is the prolife vocation of husbands and fathers. It is their path to holiness and to the perfection of charity. It is their contribution to the building of a civilization that is worthy of human dignity, a civilization of life and love.

Work and Finances

KEVIN LOWRY

The eye is the lamp of the body. So, if your eye is healthy, your whole body will be full of light; but if your eye is unhealthy, your whole body will be full of darkness. If then the light in you is darkness, how great is the darkness! (Matthew 6:22-23)

One of the most sincere compliments I have ever received in the workplace was when a female colleague said to me, "Thanks for always looking at me in the eyes." She was leaving the company after several years. We had worked together quite a bit during that time, and enjoyed a cordial, professional relationship. But this comment was personal. "I'm not sure how to say this, but I just wanted to thank you for always looking at me in the eyes when we spoke. I appreciate it."

Caught completely off guard, I managed a barely coherent "You're welcome" before we said goodbye and parted ways.

Later that day, I was working on a project with my good friend and colleague John, a fellow Christian and married man. We had often discussed how to best live our faith in the workplace, and I knew him as an individual of conviction—and discretion. Still a little astonished, I decided to mention the comment from earlier in the day.

"Oh, that's not surprising at all. Someone told me that she's had breast implants, and a couple guys in the office didn't do a very good job hiding their interest in her appearance."

Wow. I felt embarrassed for my female colleague, realizing that we had shared the same workplace, but a completely different work environment.

Cause and effect

As a married man with a bunch of kids, I was often grateful to be spared from the more lewd wing of the office grapevine. Yet at the same time, I'm a guy. We tend to be visual creatures, and just because we're married doesn't mean we're blind. I wasn't completely unaware of my female colleague's attractiveness. Sometimes, looking women in the eyes requires effort.

Yet isn't that effort worthwhile? Let's think about this for just a minute. What are the consequences of either making the effort, or not? Do any such consequences even exist?

Imagine for a moment what kind of impact this situation had on the office. Forget about whether the implant rumor was true or not. Let's agree that my coworker was an attractive young woman, like you'd find in countless workplaces. From a business standpoint, consider the possible ramifications of men focusing on her appearance:

➤ *It could harm relationships necessary to carry out the company's mission*

➤ *It could cause her to be self-conscious and detract from her work efforts*

➤ *It could cause distractions for fellow employees if observations were shared with others*

➤ *It could harm the company's culture by denigrating the dignity of, and objectifying, women in the office; but here's the thing: there's even more to it than the business impact. What about for Christians who are striving to live virtuous lives, including in the workplace?*

➤ *Indulging in lustful thoughts is the moral equivalent of fornication or adultery—mortal sins*

➤ *Gawking at women dishonors ourselves, them, and our wives, for those of us who are married*

➤ *It sets a terrible example for others; if our goal is to imitate Christ, we're on the wrong track*

➤ *Our actions have an impact on where and how we spend eternity; we're called to love with purity and chastity!*

The Crux of the Matter

The above situation concerning how women are treated in the workplace is just one example of how embracing our Christian faith has a practical impact on our daily work. Obviously, giving into vice has the potential to create a negative spiral that can cause unanticipated consequences. Thankfully, embracing virtue in our work can have a positive, and even more powerful effect.

In fact, our work is a source of multifaceted challenges – and opportunities. We earn a living, we work for ourselves, our customers, our families, we face difficulties, we pray, we interact with others, we strive for virtue – all in a day's work. In order for our work to have lasting value for ourselves and others around us, our faith is utterly indispensable.

We need grace, and we need a plan. Then we need to persevere, no matter what.

But strive first for the kingdom of God and his righteousness, and all these things will be given to you as well. (Matthew 6:33)

Putting God First

If our plan includes getting to heaven, we need to strive for the kingdom of God with all we are and all we do. As a result, our work takes on an entirely new meaning. I am firmly convinced that our work provides us with the opportunity to become better Catholics, as we overcome obstacles, practice a spirit of servant leadership, and strive to follow the Lord fully and completely. At the same time, I believe our faith provides us with the opportunity to become better workers, as we work for God first, putting forth our best efforts and acting in a spirit of humility. Our goal must be to act with honor, every single day, recognizing that the ramifications of our actions are broad and deep.

Create a Plan to Act with Virtue in Our Work

By way of illustration, let's return to our example of working with attractive women. We know that it's going to happen, they're everywhere. Their beauty is a gift from God, and while we hope they embrace high standards of modesty, the responsibility to act honorably is ours.

What does that look like? Of course we need to look them in the eyes. But beyond that, married or not, we also need to treat them as sisters in Christ and act like gentlemen. One of the techniques that always helped me was to hold myself to a high standard: treating other women in the workplace as I would have other men treat my wife. Call it the "rule of respect."

When we succeed in embracing the rule of respect, we honor twice, or thrice – our wives (if applicable), the women with whom we're working, and God. Remember, honoring our wives is part of the promise and vocation of husbands. In the words of St. Paul, "… husbands should love their wives as they do their own bodies. He who loves his wife loves himself. For no one ever hates his own body, but he nourishes and tenderly cares for it, just as Christ does for the church, because we are members of his body." (Ephesians 5:28-30)

Conversely, if we fail, we dishonor twice – or thrice.

Since I'm happily married to a beautiful woman, one technique I've used over time is simple: when I see an attractive woman in the workplace, I reflexively think of my wife. There are plenty of positive memories I can bring to mind instantly that helps avoid temptation and further deepen my love of my wife and appreciation for her beauty. This causes me to go home at night with a sense of satisfaction that potential temptations were handled in a way that honored my wife – and honored God.

If you're not married, think of a woman whom you respect – your mother, a sister, someone with whom you share a strong, loving – and of course non-sexual – bond. If you need even more horsepower, think of Bl. Teresa of Calcutta, or even the Blessed Virgin Mary! Then treat women in your workplace the same way you would want other men treating her.

Easier said than done, you might say? Well, sure. Again, we need grace, a plan and perseverance. So begin with prayer. Always begin with prayer. Then execute the plan, remembering to guard two things: your eyes, and your thoughts. If you need help, find someone who can give you the support you need – a priest, spiritual director, family member, counselor, whoever makes sense under the circumstances. Then persevere.

Of course, it could be that you have other particular challenges in your workplace. The same approach is applicable: pray, plan, persevere. For added objectivity, I'm a huge fan of spiritual direction (for a terrific introduction to the subject, check out my friend Dan Burke's book Navigating the Interior Life) or even career coaching from a faith perspective. Precisely because it's often so challenging, our work is one of the best opportunities we have to strengthen our faith – and simultaneously become the most effective workers possible.

Work Matters

Another challenge men often encounter is basing too much of our self-identity on what we do, rather than who we are. In a sense, this is putting the cart before the horse. Our identity as men of God should come first, and this ought to help fuel our quest to become the best we can at whatever role we currently play.

I learned this lesson the hard way. A while ago, I decided to leave the corporate world and work for a small Catholic non-profit organization. It meant a substantial pay cut, a long commute and less job security (the organization was struggling financially at the time). Yet through prayer and consultation with my spiritual director, it also seemed that the Lord was calling me in a new direction. On the plus side, there would be more family time, an opportunity to write, and perhaps an incentive to simplify a bit.

Through this experience, along with concurrent challenges in my family life (at one point we had four teenagers!) it became clear that God was working on my humility. And I needed it.

For me, finding a sense of detachment from my career turned into a very good lesson indeed. It took time, but I re-learned the value of service and doing things out of sheer love of our Lord, and others. In fact, my first book entitled *Faith at Work: Finding Purpose Beyond the Paycheck* was written during that first year out of the corporate world – because I had the time. It was as if God granted me this time as a gift, and gave me the motivation – and inspiration – to write a book of encouragement for those who seek to integrate faith and work.

Beyond that, I have learned that humility is an utterly foundational virtue. In our dealings with others, in our prayer lives, as sons, husbands, fathers – we are called to serve. We are called to self-sacrifice, to pour out our very selves for the benefit of others. We often think of big, major challenges when we think of sacrifice, but in my experience that's not usually the case. It's generally the small stuff. Yes, I'm still working on this too!

As you might imagine, the other area that took on even greater significance through this experience was that of money. Since our work and financial lives are so closely intertwined, it makes sense to also consider the subject of money in the context of our faith.

No one can serve two masters; for a slave will either hate the one and love the other, or be devoted to one and despise the other. You cannot serve God and wealth. (Matthew 6:24)

Faith and Finances

As a CPA, one of the ways I have served my family is through managing our family finances. Several years ago, I was surprised when my wife invited me to join her at a seminar at our parish dealing with personal finance. Some guy named Dave Ramsey, she said. Financial Peace University, she said.

"Seriously?" I asked, more than a little exasperated. "What am I going to learn that I don't already know?" (You can probably tell this was prior to my awakening about the importance of humility!)

Famous last words. I ended up going to the seminar. The seminar ended up being a bit more than that – it was a thirteen week study of various aspects of personal financial planning. I wasn't familiar with Dave Ramsey before that time (although I had read several books by Larry Burkett, who had a big influence on him) but I sure am now. Going through Dave's Financial Peace University course caused us to change our entire approach to finances in our family.

In a sense, I was right – I didn't learn tons of new technical stuff about finance. However, I had missed the bigger picture. What the course did was get my wife and me on the same page.

That was a minor miracle.

In the long run, it also turned into my leading more Financial Peace University courses, and later its Catholic counterpart (created by my friend Phil Lenahan) 7 Steps to Becoming Financially Free. I can't recommend these courses highly enough, they were transformative for our entire family. We established an emergency fund, got out of consumer debt (although we're still working on our mortgage) and came away with shared financial priorities.

But here's what is equally amazing: although we didn't see it coming, I wouldn't have been able to leave the corporate world if we hadn't taken that course and strengthened our family's financial position. One of the ways we did this was to consciously and prayerfully leave the path of voracious consumerism.

Consumer Training?

Part of this lesson resulted from my past stupidity. Let's face it, when it comes to money, one of the practical ways we can exercise a little humility is through how we handle family funds.

A few years ago, I went through a phase where I did pretty much the opposite.

I have always liked fast cars. When I was a kid, I read car magazines, memorizing statistics about Lamborghinis and Porsches, all the while dreaming of someday owning a sports car. During my teenage years, I had a Dodge Daytona turbo and later a Mustang GT. A friend of mine in college drove a black Corvette, and was somehow trusting enough to let me drive it from time to time. It was great.

My wife and I planned my mid-life crisis years in advance. Instead of doing something stupid, like trading in my wife for a new model, I would buy a fast car. Great plan, right? In my late 30s, I knew something was up one day when I came home and found her shopping online for cars. "It's time," she said. Within 24 hours, I bought a used Corvette.

This went on for a couple years, and during that time I went through two Corvettes and a Pontiac GTO (6.0 liter, 400 horsepower, zero to sixty in 4.7 seconds, quarter mile… well, you get the picture). It was only my occasional fits of fiscal responsibility that kept me selling them with a sigh. In the end, I had to admit to a pathological condition – nothing was ever fast enough.

So what's the problem? Shouldn't a guy be able to have some fun? Aren't hobbies acceptable, even desirable for men bearing the burden of heavy responsibilities? There's no mortal sin involved here, right?

Well sure, but our goal is higher than just avoiding mortal sin. The problem in my case is that my actions were self-indulgent at a time when we really didn't have the money to spend. We went into debt as a family to support my "hobby." I was able to rationalize it as a great way to connect with my kids (one on one time in the Corvette, I would say to myself) but all these excuses didn't make it right in the context of our budget.

There's a better way, and one that I believe helps us fulfill our masculine mission – being hard on ourselves, and more generous with others.

A friend of mine is terrific at this. He drives a modest car, dresses neatly but not ostentatiously, and instead of buying too many toys and clothes for his kids, he is involved in their activities and takes them on trips. His "indulgence" of his family consists of spending time with them, and foregoing the opportunity to make more money in favor of being present in their lives.

This approach illustrates what is really important – life isn't about money or its accumulation, it's about relationships. Our relationship with God is first, for sure, followed by our relationship with family, friends, co-workers, anyone in our orbit. We're to be Christ for these people, and that means not a life of drudgery and negative sacrifice, but rather a life of joyful gratitude for others and a desire to serve them out of love. People matter. And generosity towards others (within the boundaries of fiscal prudence) consists of the gift of our very selves.

Do not store up for yourselves treasures on earth, where moth and rust consume and where thieves break in and steal; but store up for yourselves treasures in heaven, where neither most not rust consumes and where thieves do not break in and steal. For where your treasure is, there your heart will be also. (Matthew 6:19-21)

Endless Opportunity for Eternal Treasures

As we go about our daily lives, it's important to take a small step back on a regular basis. Have you ever seen charts illustrating the "miracle" of compound interest? Perhaps you've seen this in the context of retirement planning. If you begin early in your career, and put a certain percentage of your salary into a 401(k) plan, you see it grow over the course of time to amounts that far exceed the sum of what you've contributed. Magic? No, this illustrates the power of setting a course, and staying on it day in and day out in order to achieve a tangible goal.

The same is true for our work and financial lives. If we set a course, to live our faith at work on a daily basis, to use money responsibly, and to temper our own desires in favor of serving our families and others, we can achieve even greater goals. There is endless opportunity to build eternal treasures by serving the Lord, and pouring out our very selves for the benefit of others. Interest rates go up and down, as does the market, but the Holy Spirit can multiply our humble efforts in ways that far surpass even the most optimistic compound interest chart.

Men, we need grace to make this happen. Pray. Embrace the sacraments. Have a plan. And persevere like your life depends on it. When we love, it's a joy to serve.

Heroism Survives Secularism

JARED ZIMMERER

Heroism is an aspect of humanity that seems a bit difficult to truly define but we know it when we see it. Authentic heroism spans across all ethnic, racial, and cultural barriers. Endless examples of war heroes, martyrs, or ancestors, thrill our consciousness and bid us to follow in the footsteps of the greats. Interestingly enough, in a time when rampant secularism has taken hold of modern society, heroism stands the test of change.

We find that throughout history, literature, film, and other major cultural facets heroism is consistently brought up. But what is heroism? Should we define it by acts of bravery and valor on the battlefield or by humble acts in solitude? Does heroism necessarily occur on a national scale or could a hero be someone who never left their hometown? What might be a hero to one person, may very well be a villain to another. So how should a man define what heroism is and how can these differing views come together into a unified vision?

What if I were to tell you that there was one aspect of the teachings of the western world and the eastern world on which all might agree? And that this aspect is the very heart of heroism? Setting specifically Christian teachings aside for the moment in order to revisit them as a way of approaching this theme of heroism from the secularists viewpoint, think about a few of the philosophies that have been the foundation of entire societies for centuries. In the east we have the teachings of Confucius, Buddha, and Lao-Tsu. In the west we have Socrates, Plato, and Aristotle. One unifying theme, while expressed in differing methods, between each of these teachers is that virtue, above all else, creates the definitive male. According to Douglas J. Soccio's book, *The Archetypes of Wisdom*, Confucius taught virtue in the teaching that harmony and nobility of the soul are what make life meaningful and man reaches these goals by wisdom, humanity and courage.

Siddhartha Gautama, who later called himself the Buddha, taught that serenity, non-attachment, and empathy were the key virtues. Lao-Tsu, the founder of Taoism, taught that unselfishness, humility and 'becoming like water', i.e. willingness to change, is what makes us virtuous. Now, compare that to the teachings of Socrates who taught that the seeking of truth, knowledge and self-awareness were what made life worthy. Plato who taught the four Cardinal virtues: wisdom, temperance, courage and justice. And the last of the examples, Aristotle, who had an extensive list of virtues meant to defeat the vice within our lives. Each of these teachers has in common the desire to spread the message of virtue.

Virtue is about upholding standards, the willingness to forego certain pleasures for the betterment of the individual as well as society. I believe that this is the basic tenet of heroism as well. In other words, to be a hero, one must be virtuous. This is how the ideals of heroism surpass all ethnic or religious lines because within heroism we find the delineating connection between separate belief systems. For example, when a soldier gives his life for his country, we recognize the heroism of the act because of the innate recognition of the virtues the soldier upheld, i.e. courage and justice. Heroism survives the sands of time because the virtues it displays are eternal. While each culture may have their own examples of heroic men and women, virtue binds them all.

In order to exhibit the concepts of heroism in concrete ways, the literary works of a culture have much to offer. For the purpose of this book, defining the heroic Renaissance man, I will use examples from a few works of literature that have had a large impact on me both as a reader as well as a man. Homer's *The Odyssey* is one book that every man should read. Odysseus, the heroic protagonist, displays heroism on many different levels. Odysseus' unwavering loyalty to his family is heroic in that no matter the obstacle, he fought through with the end in mind. Heroism is about more than just the fight; it is about that for which the hero fights. Odysseus fought temptations, villains, and self-doubt so that he might behold his wife and child again. The love he held in his heart was beyond any fear he might have experienced on the journey towards them. Aside from the heroic acts of bravery this is also a story of manhood. Men should have to battle for happiness and authentic love. This is how we were built. Being heroic is found in fulfilling that purpose and mission.

The next work, one of the most profound literary works of human history, is Scripture. As Christians, we believe that the Bible is indeed the inspired Word of God. The story of how God relates to mankind. However, even for the secularist, the action and heroism found in both the New and Old Testaments is breathtaking. Each of the heroes had their own strengths and weaknesses but it was in pushing through by firmly grasping what they believe in that they became heroes. Difficulties were endless: plagues, barbarians, slavery, and eccentric rules from God, were the norm, yet through their ability to hold onto a faith they became the legendary heroes that have lasted centuries. It is easy to forget the real story of many of these characters. The nursery rhymes and coloring books have done a bit of an injustice to the reality of the stories.

Take Moses for example. The picture given is a man who heard a command from God and decided to take his people away from the tyranny of Egyptian slavery. And yes, this is the basic premise of the story. However, think about the reality of what actually occurred. Moses, a simple man from the mountains, was once spoken to through the medium of a burning bush that couldn't turn to ash. Imagine after Moses came down from the mountain and explained that one to his family. Then after making the firm decision to follow through with the command, he is forced to meet with his adopted brother who should be looking for Moses to try him, and probably kill him, for the murder of a soldier. Moses was gutsy enough to continue. Then after explaining that he is there to take away all of the Hebrew slaves, the livelihood of most of Egypt, he warns the Pharaoh that God will punish him if he resists. The stage is now set for the ten renowned plagues. A river of blood, frogs, lice, wild animals, and pestilence surrounds the Pharaoh's kingdom. Boils are rotting people from the inside. Hail and locusts rain down on the inhabitants. This sounds more like a combination of Fear Factor and a dark, mythological, fantasy novel; a real hell on Earth. Finally, the two last plagues: three days of darkness and the killing of the firstborn sons of Egypt, including the son of Pharaoh. Moses had to be prepared for the inevitable backlash, but it was in his living out the virtues of justice, fortitude and prudence that he was unafraid, or at least willing to deal with the fear like a man. Moses' example is heroism for anyone who properly reads the story. Stepping into danger for the betterment of others is a major staple of heroism and indeed, the staple of authentic manhood. His leadership did not rest on full confidence of the 'how' of the mission but rather on the 'why'.

The Old Testament is riddled with amazing feats of bravery and heroism which far exceed those of the champions of today. These were dangerous and terrifying times of war, famine, and familial strife nevertheless in between the blurred lines of jeopardy men rose to the occasion and did what must be done. Our Lord endowed them with the qualities necessary to see the mission to the bitter end no matter what the cost. These men were afraid at times, they doubted but they also surrendered to the will of their Creator. They gave their lives to a higher purpose, which is what virtue is all about and without virtue you have no heroism.

To continue on the quest through scriptural literary heroes let's take a look at the New Testament. For the time being, I want to focus on the twelve apostles as I will revisit the heroism of Christ toward the end of the chapter. Imagine this scene. You are going about your duties when all of a sudden a man you've only seen around town comes up to you and challenges you to follow him. There's a quality to him that you've never seen in other men and so you decide to take the risk. As time passes and you hear more and more of this man's teachings your vision of him begins to change. You see him heal countless individuals and perform dreamlike miracles, raising a man from the dead and curing the sick and suffering with simple words. He is a man of deep prayer and devotion but he says some exceptionally off-putting remarks with no remorse or guilt in his voice, however, somehow, someway, what he says is like a shot to the heart and you can't help but believe him. Finally he asks, "Who do you say that I am?" What would your answer be?

There were eleven men who decided to answer with their undying devotion to the Son of God. Sadly, one of their brothers betrayed the man they had come to worship. The world hated their master. Those who were willing to be his followers were constantly under the threat of death. Yet after all this, these men were there for the mission. The men then set out on a quest, an adventure to spread the word of the risen Lord. The undertaking was no small thing. Most of the men gave their lives by the end of it. But to think that what these men believed was so strong within them that they were willing to travel to the four corners of the world and eventually give their lives in a gruesome and tortuous death meant that something there was worth dying for and through their deaths the adventure passed to the next generation. This is a heroism that lasts, one that can be handed down from generation to generation and always be new, always begging the person to be more than the generation before. Living out real, Catholic Christianity is heroism. We come from a long line of heroes which started with these eleven men of dignity, strength, and simplicity.

It seems that in looking through the lens of heroism scripture surpasses and multiplies the ideals of what heroism is. It's very heart beats with a challenge for the reader to become a hero themselves. We don't read scripture, scripture reads us and with the unending call to greatness our Lord begs the question, "Who do you say that I am?" If your answer is akin to what Peter gave to Christ, then the first step of the adventure has been taken and in the words of Bilbo Baggins, "It's a dangerous business, Frodo, going out of your door…You step into the Road, and if you don't keep your feet, there is no knowing where you might be swept off to."

In dealing with quests and adventures, I would be remiss if I did not now go into the mythical work that literally changed my life. By the time I was a senior in high school I might have read five entire books, most of which included R.L. Stine's *Goosebumps* series or other works which were required reading. I simply wasn't a reader. But then my senior literature teacher asked us to write our final paper on any work we wanted and with the movies coming out I decided to pick up a book by an odd man named Tolkien and the book was entitled *The Fellowship of the Ring*. I became thoroughly engrossed in its pages and would spend hours of sleepless nights pouring through until I finally read all of the three books of *The Lord of the Rings*. Because of Tolkien I became a reader and because of Tolkien I found a new and rich appreciation of the person of Christ. Tolkien's view of heroism is exceptionally traditional but permanently evergreen. It is heart-wrenching, tear-jerking realism found within a fantasy world and through his mythopoeic classic he brings each reader into the core of genuine truth, where Christ Himself reigns supreme.

The Lord of the Rings has sold over 150 million copies worldwide, to a vast range of audiences. The story is binding between culture and belief system. This is why Fr. Robert Barron has called J.R.R. Tolkien one of the most effective evangelists of the 20th century. It is through the medium of story that people are enthralled, the originality, the prose, the mesmerizing concept of language and culture, however, I believe that the core of the story, that which grips the heart and refuses to let go, is heroism. The profound displays of valor from unexpected characters lead the reader through the fields of virtue, which again can be recognized across a wide array of peoples. J.R.R. Tolkien's work is one of the most weighty examples of heroism in modern literature, people recognize its goodness and are changed internally simply by reading the pages of a book.

Literature can be a powerful tool in the building of a heroic society, one in which boys are raised to be men of virtue and honor. When reading about the valiant deeds of others, even if they might be fictional, it grips the soul and begs the question of what are you willing to die for? This causes a search for eternal truth. Secularism might be rampant today; nevertheless, a good work of literature can cause the mind to open to more than just living for the now. Rather it desires something more and oftentimes, especially with men, that search is a want to be a hero.

The revamping of comic book heroes to come to life on the big screen in new ways has been very revealing of a culture in want of purpose. These heroes have changed the hearts of young men for nearly seventy years now and they are still grabbing the collar bones of a whole new generation today, causing them to think about life through the lens of the heroic. Heroism in film is nothing new; it has been around since the beginning.

Though the heroism is displayed through different faces and action sequences the core of the story seems similar in most. A man who might still be trying to figure out what his life's purpose is realizes that he has a talent or an ability to swallow his fear. A villainous man, angry at the world, crops up out of some horrendous action of the past and decides to rain down his anger on the innocent. The hero realizes that he has been called to do his part in stopping the villain. Whether it's a battle of wits or action the climax begins and the tug and pull of hero to anti-hero ensues until finally the hero wins or at least stops the villain. We see this in the westerns, science fiction, super hero, fantasy, courtroom drama, and nearly any other genre of film where the hero can properly be identified.

These models of true heroism, which can be found within cultures from the beginning of time, are foreshadowing visions of greatness of the person of Christ and his mission. He embodies and exemplifies what a hero is: a selfless leader willing to lay his life down for those he loves. Heroism is not found in the mental capacities alone, neither in the actions of one man against another. Rather heroism is a liquid combination of all that is good, true and beautiful, i.e. virtuousness. Christianity is based upon selfless audaciousness, bidding men to lead a lifestyle worthy of the calling. What the ancient philosophers foresaw as duty and righteousness, or heroic living, Christ fulfilled and invited the entire world to join in. The image of Christ hanging on the cross is the heroic, iconic, all-enveloping image of all things manly. In his heroism he invites men to join the struggle, one of self-discipline and courage.

By adhering to the principles of heroism we become even more the New Catholic Renaissance Man. He is well versed in manners as well as the ability to defend and protect. A Renaissance Man has an interest in many fields. The motto 'Jack of all trades, Master of none' is laughable to the man with more vision than most. The New Catholic Renaissance Man has a want, almost a need, to learn about his surroundings, to know and to feel what true love is and to find out if and when it exists. He has a deep appreciation for beauty; beauty of nature, poetry, literature, and human dignity. Well versed in the Word of God and easily held accountable when one needs a friend. He holds himself at a much higher standard than he holds the others around him. Knowing of fallen human nature he has mercy and forgiveness flowing from his heart yet a stern position held upon his own manners and sinful nature. He has an extensive knowledge of how to defend himself and how to keep his body at its pinnacle. He can see the unknown through the lenses of faith, reason, and the sciences. He feels just as comfortable in a tuxedo as he does in a camouflage fatigue aiming a rifle at a white-tail buck from 100 yards away.

When a person speaks with him, that person is left with an everlasting impression of the most passionate yet humble man with the aptitude to truly listen. He is willing to pay attention to the opinions of others yet forms his own off of objective truth. He does not care about the fads of his time, all the while having more sensibility about the falsehoods of the sad, broken world that he was born into. He strives to be his best with the abilities and talents given to him from an Almighty Creator yet never wanting the fame or fortune associated with today's celebrity worshipping culture. He longs to know, love and serve something greater than he is, and that fulfillment of his desires is found within his Catholic faith.

Are there still men out there that are striving to live up to such a lofty lifestyle? Or are most men sneering at someone like this and considering his way of life a sham? Is this something that can be revived with our world? I think that it can and that true leadership into the real change that we all need depends upon it. I fear that we no longer are striving for the well rounded human being in today's society. If a person is not specialized into a field he is looked upon as a dunce. Intellectual curiosity has all but left the typical male today, as well as a deep appreciation for tradition and classical rhetoric. The ancient philosophers as well as the greatest minds of the so called 'dark ages' have left us with an everlasting ancestry of men who desire to know about their surroundings as well as why they exist. Whether it be the need for survival, a round table discussion of virtue or Bach's Mass in B minor, or leading a crowd in prayer and devotion, the real man is ready for anything, even death. It seems that men today are in great need to revive and restore the traditional values and morals of the greats. Our current society fills our curiosities with garbage and tells us that it is gold. But we have to see things for what they are, garbage can only beget more garbage, a mind filled with secularly materialistic nonsense could never write the next 'Wealth of Nations' or compose the next 'Mythopoeia'. If we are going to save our world from evil doers we have got to start with ourselves, and that, gentlemen, is true heroism.

Theology of the Body in Prayer

GERARD-MARIE ANTHONY

The following is an excerpt from Who Am I? Theology of the Body in Prayer *by Gerard-Marie Anthony and is used with permission.*

John Paul II, through his *Theology of the Body*, gives us the essential item to begin our journey by giving us our roadmap as this shows what man was made to be from the beginning. After all, our human experiences reflect invisible realities. This is the "thesis statement" of John Paul II's *Theology of the Body*, "The body, in fact, and it alone" the Pope says, "is capable of making visible what is invisible: the spiritual and divine. It was created to transfer into the visible reality of the world, the mystery hidden since time immemorial in God, and thus to be a sign of it" (Feb. 20, 1980). In other words, somehow the body enables us to 'see' spiritual realities, even the eternal mystery 'hidden' in God." Christopher West puts it marvelously as he notes:

Man simply cannot penetrate through reason alone the "great mystery" of the human body. Through reason, man can discover the workings of his own body as a biological organism, often with great precision and benefit to humanity. But the human body is not only biological. It is also, and even more so theological. Only to the degree that we know what our bodies "say" theologically do we know who we really are and therefore, how we are to live.[2]

Thus, in order to understand who we are, we have to understand not only our biological and social function (how we can fulfill our desires and benefit society), but the spiritual part of ourselves as well. It is only then that we can embrace our complete self because we embrace all three aspects of ourselves through prayer: the biological (man as seen naturally, not necessarily including his supernatural destiny), social, and theological.

---

[2] Ibid., pp. XXVIII-XXIX.

In prayer we fulfill our biological aspect in the fact that we fulfill our ultimate desire: to be loved and to love. St. Bernard of Clairvaux tells us this as he states that the basis of the prayer life is "the correct ordering of love."[3] We move from selfish love to true love which all of us deserve and desire.

Prayer fulfills our social longings because it puts us in a community of persons that help us, as Matthew Kelly so wonderfully notes, "To be holy or the best version of yourself." This community of unconditional support comes together for the purpose of love. This community is the Church and through the Church, Christ shows He is the true Emmanuel. He lets us know that "God is with us" (Matt. 1:23).[4] This aspect of wanting to be useful for society is also carried out in the act of changing this same society for the better. Could you imagine how much better society would be if everyone viewed one another in a personal light; not for what they can do, but for who they are? It would be a revolution of indescribable proportions.

Finally, prayer helps us to discover what our bodies "say theologically." This is the foundation of the Theology of the Body and key to prayer. As John Paul II states, "Through the fact that the Word of God became flesh, the body entered theology... through the main door" (Apr. 2, 1980).[5] Since Jesus took on flesh, our bodies have a theological meaning and give us a clue about who we are and what it means to be human.

A story may help explain. I once met a lady in a nursing home. We talked about many things: life, jobs, and even read Scripture together. We were really hitting it off, but then I had to leave. So as I was about to leave, I asked if she would like to pray with me. She said, "No." I thought maybe she did not hear me correctly, so I spoke louder and a little slower, "Would you like to pray with me?" She folded her arms and said, "No!" I was really taken back because we had just talked about God and even read Scripture only twenty minutes ago. I did not want to force her, but was

---

[3] Martin, Ralph. *Bernard Lives!: The Journey to God with Bernard of Clairvaux* (Ann Arbor, MI: Renewal Ministries, 2005), Disc 1.
[4] New American Bible. All quotations henceforth shall come from this translation unless otherwise noted.
[5] Christopher West. *Theology of the Body for Beginners: A Basic Introduction to Pope John Paul II's Sexual Revolution* (West Chester, PA: Ascension Press, 2004), p. 7.

curious how this "sudden change of heart" came about. So I asked her why she did not want to pray. She looked at me, unfolded her arms and said with tears in her eyes, "Because I don't know how."

We can relate to her because we all "want to be truly human" but because of sin, "don't know how." So we too have to relearn what it means to be human and to do that we have to look at original man.

Original Man is man before the fall; how we were originally intended to be, without sin, and in original happiness. We start off by noting that man (as male and female) was set apart from the other animals, "The LORD God formed man out of the clay of the ground and blew into his nostrils the breath of life, and so man became a living being" (Gen. 2:7). Man's being or life was meant to be inspired, filled with the breath/ Spirit of God. MAN IS NOT JUST ANOTHER ANIMAL (in the generic way we use it today). He is something greater because he, as then-Cardinal Joseph Ratzinger states, "is a fit habitation for God."[6] Thus, he is no longer simply an animal, but something holy or set apart. He is a person.

Thus, God gave Adam and Eve many special gifts in order to help them be an image of Himself and rest in Him. He gave him all of creation, preternatural gifts,[7] free-will, intellect, and three original experiences that man has lost. The most important gift however was grace and it built upon all the other gifts given to man. Now, as the story continues, we see that man gains his knowledge, makes decisions, and experiences things from his senses. From his senses, he realizes that he is not like the other animals. Genesis points out, "The man gave names to all the cattle, all the birds of the air, and all the wild animals; but none proved to be the suitable partner for the man" (Gen. 2:20). This

---

[6] Joseph Cardinal Ratzinger and Hans Urs Von Balthasar. *Mary -The Church at the Source* (San Francisco: Ignatius Press, 2005), p. 66.

[7] John Hardon, *Modern Catholic Dictionary* (Garden City, NY: Doubleday and Company, Inc., 1980), p.437. PRETERNATURAL GIFTS-Favors granted by God above and beyond the powers or capacities of the nature that receives them but not beyond those of all created nature. Such gifts perfect nature but do not carry it beyond the limits of created nature. They include three great privileges to which human beings have no title--infused knowledge, absence of concupiscence, and bodily immortality. Adam and Eve possessed these gifts before the Fall.

experience is known as original solitude and we can all relate to this. At first, you think, "Hey I'm special. I'm not like anyone else." This is why we put on the special cologne or perfume, why women hate having the same outfits at formals. We want to be unique. This is one aspect of solitude. At the same time however, we feel, "I'm all alone in the world. I cannot relate to anyone. Nobody understands me. I just want someone to love." This is the second aspect of original solitude. Pope John Paul II refers to this in his *Theology of the Body*:

Thus, the created man finds himself from the first moment of his existence before God in search of his own being, as it were; one could say, in search of his own definition; today one would say, in search of his own "identity." The observation that man "is alone" in the midst of the visible world and, in particular among living beings, has a negative meaning in this search, inasmuch as it expresses what man "is not." Nevertheless, the observation that he cannot identify himself essentially with the visible world of other living beings (animalia) has, at the same time, a positive aspect for the primary search: even if this observation is not yet a complete definition, it nevertheless constitutes one of its elements.[8]

So trying to discover who we are and even asking God the questions "what" or "why" is not something evil or bad. It is searching for the answers to the question of "Who am I," just like original man. Hence, we see that original solitude, "refers not only to Adam's experience of being 'alone' without a helper, but also to the human experience of being 'alone' in the visible world as a person made in God's image and likeness. Adam discovered his solitude by naming the animals and realizing he was fundamentally different from them."[9] Therefore, solitude means uniqueness as a person.

The realization that we are not like the other living creatures and our longing not to be alone brings us to what Pope John Paul II terms original unity. Man has a longing to be a gift to someone. You hear it in every song, see it in every movie, and read it in every story. We all want to give ourselves to someone. Thus, our

---

[8] John Paul II, *Theology of the Body*, 5:5
[9] West, *Theology for Beginners*, p. 131.

bodies tell us something theologically if we listen to this yearning. This yearning to be a gift is known as the nuptial meaning of the body. It "refers to the call to love as God loves inscribed in the human body as male and female. If we live according to the nuptial meaning of our bodies, we fulfill the very meaning of our being and existence."[10] This is why Adam exclaims, "This one, at last, is bone of my bones and flesh of my flesh" (Gen. 2:23). We can all relate to the feeling of finding someone we can love and who loves us back. This love or unity in the beginning was between God and man, man and woman, and mankind and creation. A three-fold love to image the three-fold love within God: First, as individual Persons "for God is love" (1Jn. 4:8); Second, as community since He is three Persons in one God and consequently a community of love; and third, as a love for His Creation, especially mankind, because "God looked at everything he had made, and he found it very good" (Gen. 1:31). Therefore, Original Unity "refers to man and woman's experience of self-donating love and communion prior to sin. This unity eased man's solitude in the sense of being without a 'helper,' but affirmed human solitude in the sense of being different from the animals."[11]

The last original experience is Original Nakedness. This "refers to the original experience of nakedness without shame. Adam and Eve were untainted by shame because they had no experience whatsoever of lust."[12] Adam and Eve saw each other for who they really were, not simply on a superficial, functional level. They were free to truly be themselves because they knew the other loved him or her unconditionally. Hence, Scripture says, "The man and his wife were both naked, yet they felt no shame" (Gen. 2:25).

All of these experiences are crucial to understanding and developing the prayer life and becoming the person that God has made us to be. We will come back to them again and again as we follow our roadmaps to lasting happiness, i.e. holiness. St. Teresa

---

[10] West, *Theology for Beginners*, p. 133.
[11] Ibid., p. 131.
[12] Ibid., p. 132.

of Avila describes holiness when she says, "our whole welfare consists in doing the will of God," [13] thus having our wills in line with God's will. She continues, "We can only learn to know ourselves and do what we can: namely, surrender our will and fulfill God's will in us." [14] What is God's will? It is for us to be the person that He made us to be. He does not make us as accidents or so we can hide our personalities. He tells us the exact opposite:

You are the light of the world. A city set on a mountain cannot be hidden. Nor do they light a lamp and then put it under as bushel basket; it is set on a lamp stand, where it gives light to all the house. Just so, your light must shine before others, that they may see your good deeds and glorify your Heavenly Father (Matt. 5:14-16).

Thus, in being ourselves (our true selves—not the self which has been degraded by sin), we become holier and fall deeper and deeper in the love we are made for. We must dare to fall in love! So holiness "refers to the state of a person who loves rightly. God's holiness is manifested in his eternal exchange of self-giving love. Human holiness is what enables us to mirror God through the sincere gift of self. For the human person, as for the Incarnate Christ, holiness is manifested in and through the human body."[15]

Thus, from the original experiences expressed in John Paul II's *Theology of the Body*, we see that we are unique before God (original solitude), made for relationships and consequently have a nuptial meaning to our bodies. Hence, as persons, we are made to be gifts (original unity), and meant to be loved and love in truth by being who we are (original nakedness).

Prayer reflects this as well. It is the unique way that God has a relationship with us, built on the truth of whom He is as God and who we are as human persons. We are the Father's precious sons and daughters. St. Paul tells us this in his letter to the Galatians, "As proof that you are children, God sent the spirit of his Son into our hearts, crying out 'Abba, Father!' So you are no longer a slave but a child, and if a child then also an heir, through God"

---

[13] Teresa of Avila, trans. E. Allison Peers. *Way of Perfection* (New York: Image/Doubleday Books,1991), p.66.
[14] Ibid.

[15] West, *Theology for Beginners*, p. 133.

(Gal. 4:6-7). We are the dearly beloved of the Son as members of His Bride, the Church. Again, St. Paul tells us, "Husbands, love your wives, even as Christ loved the church and handed himself over for her" (Eph. 5:25). Finally, we are the dwelling place and temple of the Holy Spirit. In the First Letter to the Corinthians it says, "Do you not know that your body is the temple of the Holy Spirit within you, whom you have from God, and that you are not your own? For you have been purchased at a price. Therefore glorify God in your body" (1Cor. 6: 19-20).

Thus, we see prayer is based on truth, relationship, and love. It is the way God meets us in our human experiences and takes us to happiness. It is the way He helps us to rediscover what sin has made us forget: that we are each someone loved by God and He is grateful to call us His own. John Paul II and our bodies are the roadmap for helping us to rediscover this great mystery. So let us follow the road to happiness and begin our journey in prayer.

WOMAN: BONE OF OUR BONES

JIM BURNHAM

DAVE DINUZZO

Mary: World's Greatest Warrior, Intercessor and Mother

JIM BURNHAM

"Majestic and Heavenly Maid, Lady, Queen, protect and keep me under your wing lest Satan ... be victorious against me." –St. Ephraim (c. 306-373)

In 1862, St. John Bosco had a remarkable dream. He saw the Catholic Church as a mighty flagship in the midst of a pitched battle. Smaller enemy ships were bombarding it with books and pamphlets, bombs and cannons, and trying to ram it off course. At the same time, huge waves and fierce winds buffeted the flagship. At the helm, the Pope strained every muscle to steer his ship between two mighty columns in the sea. On the biggest, highest column was a large Host. On the other mighty column stood a statue of the Blessed Virgin Mary. In spite of all adversity, the Pope anchored the flagship to thick chains hanging from the two columns. At that, the enemy ships panicked and fled, while the wind and seas grew calm.

St. John Bosco explained that the Church will endure severe trials and persecutions. The Church's adversaries will do their utmost to destroy her. But two things will preserve the Church in that hour: frequent Communion and devotion to Mary.

The Two Pillars

You already know that the Universal Church is experiencing an all-out assault by forces natural and demonic, by foes within the Church and without. But do you realize that those same enemies are also seeking to destroy the *domestic church*—your family—in your own home? The key to surviving this attack is the same for both the Church Universal and the Church Domestic: holding fast to Jesus in the Blessed Sacrament of the Eucharist, and clinging to Mary, our heavenly Mother and Queen.

To win a war, you need two things: the best *offense* and the best *defense*. The Eucharist is obviously the best offense. The body, blood, soul and divinity of the eternal warrior King Jesus has the power to vanquish the triple-threat of the world, the flesh, and the devil. Jesus in the Eucharist is a divine weapon that overcomes all enemies, natural and supernatural.

And Mary is the best defense. Scripture says, "Put on the *full* armor of God." The Eucharist gives us the spiritual energy to fight. But to be fully protected against the wickedness and snares of the devil, we need to wrapped in the same armor with which the Warrior King himself was wrapped—the loving protection of his earthly mother. Mary is an essential part of God's full armor. She is the sinless one, the Immaculate Conception whose chink-less armor the devil can never penetrate. God created her to have maximum protection against the bullets of Satan and sin. Mary is a spiritual bullet-proof vest. Only a fool would walk into a firefight without one. If you want to save your family, teach them to embrace Jesus in the Eucharist and Mary as their spiritual mother and protector. The fundamental importance of devotion to our Lord in the Eucharist has been well explained in chapter [chapter on Eucharist]. Let us turn to the second pillar of survival: devotion to our Lady.

There's Something About Mary

For many non-Catholics, Mary is a huge stumbling block. They wonder if Catholic beliefs about Mary are biblical. They think we Catholics "make too much of Mary," that we give her too much attention, taking away from the honor we owe to Christ. As one anti-Catholic writer put it: "This most blessed of women, the mother of Jesus, is thus made His chief rival and competitor for the loyalty and devotion of the human heart."[16]

Some Catholics have misgivings about devotion to Mary. So here's the glorious truths we need to share with Catholics and non-Catholics alike: (1) *Mary and Jesus are not in competition, but are members of the same team. Mary is the first and best Christian who only leads us closer to her Son. (2) Mary's privileges all come exclusively from God and are for our benefit. (3) Mary's role in salvation is taught from Genesis to*

---

[16] Lorraine Boettner, *Roman Catholicism* (Phillipsburg, NJ: Presbyterian and Reformed Publishing, 1962) 146.

Revelation and she is, by God's design, the spiritual mother and protector of all Christians.

It's said that behind every great man is a great woman. That's definitely true of Jesus. Behind the greatest Warrior *King*, Our Lord, is the greatest Warrior *Queen*, Our Lady. This most gracious and humble of women, this simple Jewish maid, this first and best follower of Jesus, was called and equipped by God to fulfill the most awesome role ever given to a creature: to be God's mom.

This is Mary's first and greatest privilege, from which all her other privileges flow. To prepare a fitting vessel for the Incarnate Son who took his nature from Mary, God kept her free from all sin from conception onward (Immaculate Conception). To preserve Mary's *physical* intactness—as a sign of her much more valuable *spiritual* intactness—God kept her a virgin before, during, and after childbirth (Perpetual Virginity) and kept her body from decay by taking her into heaven at her life's end (Bodily Assumption).

As Catholics, we recognize that the privileges God gave the Blessed Virgin Mary are gifts for the whole human race. Mary is, in the poet Wordsworth's words, "our tainted nature's solitary boast." Her purity and obedience of faith is our model and hope. Where she dwells in sinless glory, we hope to follow. But it goes beyond that. Mary is not only Mother of the *Redeemer,* but she is also Mother of the *Redeemed*, the spiritual mother of all for whom Jesus died.

Making Mary the sinless, perpetually-virgin, bodily assumed, mother of God wasn't just for Christ's benefit. It's also for the benefit of those who follow Christ. God kept Mary physically and spiritually intact for two reasons: (1) to be a fitting mother of the Redeemer; and (2) to be a fitting mother of the Redeemed. These four defined dogmas are part of God's plan to give Mary maximum spiritual power against the powers of darkness. It was to help her fulfill her final role as the spiritual mother of all Christians, as the Warrior Queen who protects them until the end of time.

When we receive Christ as Savior, not only do we get to call his heavenly father, "Our Father" as he taught in that glorious prayer, we also get to call his earthly mother, "Our mother" as he told us, through the beloved disciple, on the cross: "*Woman, behold your son. Son,* behold your *mother*" (John 19:26-27). Aren't we all beloved disciples, or supposed to be? Aren't we all called to behold his mother as our mother? Before he shed the last drop of his blood, Jesus gave us the gift of his incomparable mother. God's mom is also our mom. So we can call Mary "our mother." But aren't Catholics making a mountain out of a molehill? Aren't we giving Mary a greater role than Scripture gives her? Not a bit. Mary's role as Warrior Queen and Mother of all Christians is taught throughout the Bible, from Genesis all the way to Revelation. But to see it, we must read the Bible as the first Christians did—in terms of types.

Previews of Coming Attractions

What are *types*? What we see—or wish we could see—before every movie: *previews* of coming attractions. The Old Testament (OT) prepared the way for the New Testament (NT). Many things in the OT are previews of even greater things in the NT. These OT people and events foreshadow, prefigure, anticipate, or symbolize their NT fulfillments. According to an ancient Christian saying: "the New Testament lies hidden in the Old and the Old Testament is unveiled in the New" (*Catechism of the Catholic Church* [hereafter *CCC*], 129).

These OT persons and events that prefigure NT persons and events are called "types." A type is a prophetic *foreshadowing* of a NT fulfillment. The *CCC* has a brief but excellent section on OT types in numbers 128–130. To fully understand the OT, we must read it in terms of types. Typology shows many NT doctrines, including Mary's privileges and roles, clearly revealed in the OT. Once a non-Catholic understands the meaning and importance of OT types, he will discover that *all* Catholic beliefs about Mary are found in the Bible. But isn't typology just reading things into the text that aren't really there? No, the NT *requires* us to read the OT in a typological sense:[17]

- *In Matthew 12:40, Jesus teaches that Jonah's three days in the belly of the great fish foreshadowed Jesus' three days in the tomb.*
- *In John 3:14, Jesus says the bronze serpent of Numbers 21:9 symbolized His crucifixion.*
- *1 Peter 3:19–21, St. Peter points out the flood in the time of Noah prefigured Christian baptism.*
- *In Romans 5:14, St. Paul specifically calls Adam a type of Christ.*

Thus, the NT teaches that in the OT people and events, we should recognize doctrines that are made more explicit in the gospel. Thus, to be faithful to the NT, we must appreciate the rich typology found in the OT. In the OT, there are three major *types* of Mary: Eve, the first woman; the Ark of the Covenant; and the Queen Mother. Together, these three great prefigures of Mary support all our Marian beliefs and devotions.

Mary as the Second Eve

The early Church Fathers made rich use of typology. Romans 5:14 teaches that Adam was a type of Christ. The Fathers realized other individuals involved in the Fall had NT counterparts. The devil, a fallen angel, brought words of death to Eve; the angel Gabriel brought words of life to Mary. Eve, our mother in the flesh, disobeyed God and contributed to Adam's sin, which caused the fall of the human race. Mary obeyed God and contributed to Christ's redemptive mission. She was his mother and perfect disciple. The Fathers made the obvious connection: just as Christ is the *new Adam* (1 Corinthians 15:45), Mary is the *new Eve*. After Adam and Eve had sinned, Genesis prophesies a woman and her son who will be at total enmity with the serpent (Satan) and his descendents: "I will put enmity between you and the woman, and

---

[17] Obviously, we must first read the Bible in a literal sense. All the other senses of Scripture typological, moral, and analogical—are based upon the literal. See *CCC*, 115–118. For more, check out Mark Shea's *Making Senses Out of Scripture* (Dallas, TX: Basilica Press, 1999).

between your offspring and hers; He will strike at your head, while you strike at his heel" Genesis 3:15 (New American Bible).

The woman's *son* will crush the serpent's head. Since the man who ultimately crushes the serpent's head is obviously *Jesus*, the woman must be his mother, Mary. Thus, Genesis 3:15–17 describes two teams: the fall team—Adam and Eve, and the redemption team—Jesus and Mary, the new Adam and new Eve. The earliest Church Fathers, such as St. Justin,[18] St. Irenaeus,[19] and Tertullian[20] were quick to realize this. Although the human race fell through Adam, Eve's role was crucial. Jesus redeemed the human race, but Mary's role was likewise crucial. As we will see in the following section, Sacred Scripture continually shows *Jesus and Mary together* in the pivotal events of our salvation.

Head-Crushing By Righteous Women

A quick overview of the Bible confirms that Jesus and Mary together will crush Satan's head. Notice how the OT describes righteous women (types of Mary) who crush Israel's enemies (types of Satan). Ever wondered why, throughout the OT, everybody seems to pick on the Jews? It's part of Satan's strategy to avoid having his head crushed. Remember, he was right there at Genesis 3:15 when God prophesied that the son of a righteous woman would crush Satan's head.

With his angelic intelligence, Satan must have devised a counter-plan that went something like: "How can I thwart this prophecy? If I kill the *son* before he crushes my head, I win. But what if he's too strong? Then I could kill the weaker *woman* before

---

[18] "[Jesus] became Man by the virgin so that the course which was taken by disobedience in the beginning through the agency of the serpent, might be also the very course by which it would be put down. For Eve, a virgin and undefiled, conceived the word of the serpent, and bore disobedience and death. But the virgin Mary received faith and joy when the angel Gabriel announced to her the glad tidings.... And she replied: 'Be it done unto me according to thy word.'" (St. Justin Martyr, *Dialogue with Trypho the Jew*, 100 [c. AD 155].

[19] "Just as [Eve] ... having become disobedient, was made the cause of death for herself and for the whole human race; so also Mary, ... being obedient, was made the cause of salvation for herself and the whole human race. ... Thus, the knot of Eve's disobedience was loosed by the obedience of Mary. What the virgin Eve had bound in unbelief, the virgin Mary loosed through faith."(St. Irenaeus, *Against Heresies*, 3,22,4 [c. AD 190].

[20] "While Eve was still a virgin ... the word of the devil crept in to erect an edifice of death. Likewise, through a Virgin, the Word of God was introduced to set up a structure of life. Thus, what had been laid waste in ruin by this sex, was by the same sex re-established in salvation. Eve had believed the serpent; Mary believed Gabriel. That which the one destroyed by believing, the other, by believing, set straight." (Tertullian, *The Flesh of Christ* 17, 5 [c. AD 210].

she gives birth. No woman, no son; no son, no head-crushing—I win. But what if she's protected or hidden? Then I could destroy God's righteous *people* before the righteous woman is born. No chosen people, no woman; no woman, no son; no son, no head-crushing. I win!" If Satan can wipe out the Jews, then he can foil God's plan of redemption.

So many times in the OT, Satan raises up evil men (types of Satan) with armies to destroy the Jews, God's chosen people. But God raises up righteous women (types of Mary) to humble and crush these types of Satan as previews of the final prophetic head-crushing. In Judges 4:17-22, Jael drives a tent peg through the skull of the Canaanite general, Sisera. Judges 5:24 celebrates her: "Most blessed of women be Jael." Whoa! Does that ring any bells? Judges 9:50-55 describes a unnamed woman who drops a millstone on the head of tyrannical King Abimelech, fracturing his skull. Judith delivers the Jewish people from the Assyrian army by beheading its commander-in-chief, Holofernes, with his own sword as he slept (Judith 12-13). Judith's heroism is celebrated with the words: "you are blessed by the Most High God *above all women on earth*; and blessed be the Lord God … who has guided you to *strike the head* of the leader of our enemies" (Judith 13:18).

The praises of Jael and Judith both anticipate Elizabeth's praise of Mary: "Blessed are you among women" (Luke 1:42). Notice that Elizabeth connects Mary with Jesus by immediately adding, "and blessed is the fruit of your womb!"

Do women do all the head-crushing? No, David (a type of Jesus, who is the son of David) defeated the Philistine champion Goliath and lopped off his head with the giant's own sword (1 Samuel 17:41-58). Thus, in the OT, types of *both* Mary and Jesus (the woman and her seed) are shown crushing types of Satan.

Jesus and Mary Together Crush Satan's Head

Jesus definitively crushed Satan's head on Calvary. Significantly, all four evangelists tell us that Calvary means "skull-place." Satan struck Jesus a supposedly deadly blow on the cross, but it proved to be a minor wound ("you strike at his heel"), or as Monty Python would say in a British accent: "merely a flesh wound."

Satan suffered the mortal blow ("he will strike at your head") as Jesus destroyed the power of sin and death. Who was at Christ's side on Calvary? *Mary.* What does Jesus call her? *"Woman."* Why? Mary is the New Eve who cooperates with the New Adam to redeem the human race. She is the cosmically-important "woman" prophesied in Genesis 3:15. Jesus also calls Mary "woman" in John 2 when he started his public ministry at her request. This was no sign of disrespect—Jesus kept all the commandments perfectly including "honor your mother." He was calling Mary the New Eve, the new woman, the righteous mother of the head-crushing son. Jesus calls her "woman" again in John 19 on the cross as he fulfills his ministry and crushes Satan on Skull-Place. Mary was with Jesus, cooperating with him, from beginning to end, from his Incarnation to his Passion,[21] to the birth of his Church at Pentecost.[22]

Mary is called "woman" one more time: in Revelation 12, describing how Mary will, along with her son Jesus, battle Satan until the end of time. From Genesis to Revelation, the Bible describes Jesus and Mary together crushing the serpent's head. It's not Jesus OR Mary. It's Jesus AND Mary. The New Adam and the New Eve are on the same victorious team. Just as Eve was the mother of the human race in the order of *nature*, now Mary—the New Eve—is the new mother of the human race in the order of *grace.*

Mary as Ark of the New Covenant

The Ark was the holiest object in the OT religion.[23] It was sacred because it carried the stone tablets of the Law that God gave

---

[21] Mel Gibson's brilliant film, *The Passion of the Christ* (2004), has a profound scene in which Mary and Satan lock eyes in silent mortal combat as they accompany Jesus to Calvary.

[22] It's no accident that the first descent of the Holy Spirit on Mary resulted in the birth of Christ, and the second descent of the Holy Spirit on Mary resulted in the birth of Christ's Church (Acts 1 and 2). This highlights Mary's twin roles as physical mother of the Savior and spiritual mother of the Saved.

[23] In addition to being the holiest object in the OT, the Ark was also the most powerful. As the Jews crossed into Canaan, the waters of the Jordan miraculously parted before the Ark allowing the people to pass over on dry ground (Joshua 3:15-17). The Jews carried the Ark before them as they conquered the land. They even collapsed the mighty walls of Jericho by merely circling it with the Ark and blowing horns (Joshua 6).

Moses at Mount Sinai. In Exodus 25, God gave meticulous instructions for constructing the Ark. It had to be made of acacia wood (supposedly incorruptible), plated inside and outside with pure gold. It had to be kept free from all impurity and profanation. In 2 Samuel 6:6-7, God struck a man named Uzzah dead because he dared to touch the Holy Ark. From the earliest centuries, Christians saw the OT Ark as a type of Mary.[24] The connection is obvious. That Ark carried the *written* Word of God; Mary carried the *living* Word. Mary is the living Ark of the living Word.

Luke draws four parallels between the OT Ark and Mary: (1) As the Ark is *overshadowed* by the glory cloud in Exodus 40:34-35, Mary is *overshadowed* by the Holy Spirit (Luke 1:35). (2) As the Ark spent *three months* in Obededom's house (2 Samuel 6:11), Mary spent *three months* in Zechariah's and Elizabeth's house (Luke 1:26, 40). (3) As King David asked: "How can the <u>ark</u> *of the Lord come to me*?" (2 Samuel 6:9), Elizabeth asked Mary: "why is this granted to me, that the <u>mother</u> *of my Lord should come to me*?" (Luke 1:43). (4) As David *leaped* and danced when the Ark arrived in Jerusalem (2 Samuel 6:14-16), John the Baptist *leaped* for joy in Elizabeth's womb when Mary arrived (Luke 1:44).

Mary is the NT fulfillment of the OT Ark. God took special care to preserve the Ark from all impurity and corruption because it carried his *written* Word. We would expect God to take even greater care to keep the NT Ark, Mary, free from all impurity and corruption since her womb carried his *living* Word. God keeps his Ark intact. God preserved Mary's virginity during childbirth, and kept her sinless and "full of grace." It follows that God would preserve Mary from bodily corruption at her life's end. Thus, the Ark helps us to see the biblical basis for doctrines like the

---

[24] For example, a 4th-century bishop, St. Maximus of Turin, details several ways the Ark of the Covenant (Ex 26:33, 40:20) prefigured Mary: "What would we say the ark was if not Holy Mary, since the ark carried within it the tables of the covenant, while Mary bore the master of the same covenant? The one bore the law within itself and the other the gospel, but the ark gleamed within and without with the divine radiance of gold, while holy Mary shone within and without with the splendor of virginity; the one was adorned with earthly gold, the other with heavenly" (Sermon 42, 5). Boniface Ramsey, O.P., *The Sermons of St. Maximus of Turin* (Mahwah, NJ: Paulist Press, 1989) 107.

Assumption, which are not taught *explicitly* in Sacred Scripture, but which are taught *implicitly* through typology.[25]

Mary as Christ's Queen Mother

The OT kings clearly prefigured Jesus Christ, the NT King of kings (Revelation 19:16). Jesus, in His humanity, descended from King David. Therefore, the kings of Judah, who were from David's line, especially prefigure Jesus' kingship. Luke 1:32: the Lord God will give to him [Jesus] the throne of his father David. Interestingly, the king of Judah's *wife* was *not* the queen. The queen was the king's *mother*. She was known as the Queen Mother. She had great honor and authority in the kingdom.

1 Kings 2:19-20: So Bathseba went to King Solomon, to speak to him on behalf of Adonijah. And the king rose to meet her, and bowed down to her; then he sat on his throne, and had a seat brought for the king's mother; and she sat on his right. Then she said, "I have one small request to make of you; do not refuse me." And the king said to her: "Make your request, my mother; for I will not refuse you."[26] Queen Mother had an official position; she had to be deposed in order to be removed (1 Kings 15:13). The Jewish idea of Davidic kings would have naturally included the king on his throne with the queen mother at his right hand. The Holy Spirit, in leading the OT people of Judah to establish the office of Queen Mother, was preparing the way for Mary. Jesus, the NT Davidic King, does not have a wife. His mother would be the NT queen.

This is exactly what Revelation 11 and 12 describe. A woman (Mary) gives birth to a son (Jesus) who will "rule all the nations" (12:5). Jesus is a new Solomon. Just as Solomon ruled over other kings (2 Chronicles 9:23–26), Jesus is the "King of kings and Lord of lords" (Revelation 19:16). Just as Solomon, son of David, built

---

[25] In Revelation 11:19-12:1, after seeing a vision of the Ark of the covenant in heaven, John immediately describes a "woman clothed with the sun" who gives "birth to a son who was to rule all the nations with an iron rod." The son is Jesus (Revelation 19:15-16), making this woman Mary. John isn't giving us the location of the lost Ark (Jeremiah 3:15-19; 2 Maccabees 1:4-8). Rather, he is describing Mary as the NT Ark, and telling us that Mary, with her "feet" and "head," is in heaven bodily.

[26] In this particular case, Solomon did refuse his mother's request because it would have caused civil war.

a Temple housing the Ark of the Covenant (the Temple was destroyed and the Ark lost in 587 BC), Jesus, son of David, builds an eternal Temple housing a new Ark of the Covenant in heaven (11:19). And just as King Solomon enthroned his queen mother at his right hand, Jesus enthrones Mary as His Queen Mother: Revelation 12:1: a woman clothed with the sun, with the moon under her feet, and on her head a crown of twelve stars.

Any king of the house of David would be expected to have a queen mother. That's precisely what Mary is: the Queen Mother of the Messianic King. Jesus is King and Lord of all creation. And Mary is the mother of the Lord, just as Elizabeth hailed her: "the *mother of my Lord*" (Luke 1:43). Thus, St. John Damascene writes: When she became Mother of the Creator, she truly became Queen of every creature."[27] By studying the great honor and dignity queen mothers had in the OT, we can appreciate the profound role God has given Mary as the NT Queen Mother.

Mary as Spiritual Mother and Protector

What does this glorious Queen Mother do? For starters, she brings us Jesus. She also perfectly does God's will—"let it be to me according to your word" (Luke 1:38)—and tells us to the do the same, just as she told the wedding servants at Cana: "Do whatever he tells you" (John 2:5). But Mary's role goes beyond being "Theotokos"—God Bearer—and beyond being an exemplar of Christian obedience. As Queen of the eternal King, Mary is called to be the spiritual mother and protector of all in his kingdom. Revelation lays out her mission: "Then the dragon was angry with the woman, and went off to make war on the rest of her offspring, on those who keep the commandments of God and bear testimony to Jesus" (Revelation 12:17).

Mary, "the woman who had borne the male child" (Revelation 12:13) has *other offspring*: those who keep God's commandments and bear witness to Jesus. That's all Christians. Mary is therefore the spiritual mother of all Christians and her role until the end of time is to stand in the gap between us and the dragon, Satan. She

---

[27] St. John Damascene, *De fide orthodoxa*, 1, 4, 14.

is the unceasing Warrior Queen behind the unceasing Warrior King. Her role—until the end of time—is to protect the spiritual Body of Christ, the Church, just as she protected the physical body of the Christ-child.

Real Men Love Their Mother

Why are Catholics devoted to Mary? Because we recognize that Mary's privileges come from God, and that we're called to celebrate God's works. *God* made Mary the world's greatest warrior and intercessor; *God* gave her to us as our mother. And like any good mother, Mary uses all her privileges to help her children—us. Catholic devotion to Mary is simply celebrating what God has done for our spiritual mother, and asking for her protection and intercession.

Scripture tells us: "Your adversary the devil prowls around like a roaring lion, seeking someone to devour" (1 Peter 5:8). Have you ever seen a lion chasing down his prey? It's a horrific sight. Do you want to be the trailing antelope as Satan pounces upon you and rips you apart? Do you want your children, or your grandchildren, to walk alone and unprotected against his deadly aggression?

Then don't be a Lone Ranger. Recognize reality. Celebrate Mary's God-given privileges. Embrace Mary as your true spiritual mother and protector. Entrust yourself and your family to the New Eve, the world's greatest woman and head-crushing warrior. Petition the King of Kings through her unfailing intercession, for he will never refuse his Queen Mother. March behind her as the unconquerable Ark of the NT Covenant. Wrap yourself in the impenetrable armor of her Immaculate Conception. Be a faithful son to Mary, and she will be to you a faithful and protective mother. Here are some practical ways to increase your devotion to Our Lady:

- *Receive Jesus in the Holy Eucharist frequently, daily if possible, and go to Confession regularly.*
- *Pray the Angelus—that great traditional prayer of the Incarnation—every day at noon.*

- *Pray her Rosary daily, meditating on the life of Christ through the heart of Mary, for no creature knew or loved him better.*
- *Wear the scapular, our Warrior Queen's colors, along with a Miraculous Medal.*
- *Say a travelling prayer (such as a Hail Mary) every time you hop in the car, asking for Mary's intercession and protection.*
- *Consecrate your family to the Sacred Heart of Christ and the Immaculate Heart of Mary.*
- *Visit an approved Marian shrine.*
- *Read good books about Mary to your children.*

Through your example, show your children how to love, honor, and imitate Mary. See your faith and your family thrive—not just survive. Watch as, little-by-little, you start to overcome the world, the flesh, and the devil. Watch as you grow in purity of thought, strength of virtue, and obedience of faith. Watch as you become a better imitator of Christ. Watch your efforts to fight alongside the Warrior King and for his kingdom, your struggle to win souls and conquer the culture of death, multiply beyond all expectation. Watch how, as you draw closer to Our Lady, she brings you ever-closer to Our Lord. So, man up, and embrace God's plan for your victory: Jesus AND Mary, together forever.

"O Mary, conceived without sin, pray for us who have recourse to thee!"

"No one has access to the Almighty as His mother has; none has merit such as hers. Her Son will deny her nothing that she asks; and herein lies her power. While she defends the Church, neither height nor depth, neither men nor evil spirits, neither great monarchs, nor craft of man, nor popular violence, can avail to harm us; for human life is short, but Mary reigns above, a Queen forever." ~ Blessed John Henry Newman

The Evils of Pornography and How to Fight It

DAVE DINUZZO SR.

I have very few strong memories from my childhood, but I can remember one quite vividly. I was ten years old and alone in the family room. I stumbled onto a sex show on one of the premium channels. We didn't have those channels in our home, just a blurry signal that day. That's all it took. I watched intently at the sexual things that were going on in front of my eyes, anxious about what I was seeing, while at the same time enthralled, having never seen anything like it before. I remember sitting right up next to the TV (we didn't have a remote back then) so I could have the volume down low and turn the channel quickly should someone come downstairs. I was confused and amazed. I knew that what I was seeing wasn't good for me, but I couldn't look away. I watched for what seemed like hours, although in reality, it was probably only a matter of twenty minutes. After viewing that pornographic show, I began experimenting with my body in a sexual way and was completely confused by what was happening with me physically. I was only ten years old… I shouldn't have been exposed to this. Nonetheless, I was exposed and that exposure set the stage for my addiction.

The subject matter contained in this chapter is often referred to as taboo. It is rare for us to hear much about the true nature of addiction to pornography and masturbation. It is even more rare for a lay-minister, who also happens to be a husband and father, to divulge the details of his "porn story." Be that as it may, I believe that the Church needs to talk about porn more openly, because the secular world certainly is talking about it. Porn should not be a silent topic. Men, women, and children need help. They are fighting for their lives with no one to come to their aid because these sins are kept private and hidden. This horrific problem must be brought into the light so that God's grace and mercy can shower upon the many that fail with the sins related to pornography use, as well as those who are abused, degraded, trafficked, pimped, infected, and even killed for its profit. A great number of people, even those who do not currently look at, use, buy, or sell porn, believe that there is nothing wrong with porn. This is a sign of a culture that has completely and utterly lost its moral compass.

The porn industry portrays itself as alluring, glamorous, luxurious, and as something "everybody does." It tells males that in order to be a "real man", they must look at porn, and that it is completely natural. It makes men believe that it's normal to consume incredibly large doses of smut, lust, and obscenity, and that somehow that makes males more manly. These are lies. We were created for greatness, not for mediocrity and what "everybody else is doing". We're called to stand and defend, especially against sly predators, which porn most certainly is. It's not that porn is only bad for me and for some other select group of people. It's not that I'm 'trying to force my morality on someone'. It's not that only certain kinds of porn are bad; it's all intrinsically evil. The *Catechism of the Catholic Church*, paragraph 2354, states: "It (pornography) offends against chastity because it perverts the conjugal act... It does grave injury to the dignity of its participants... It is a grave offense." The production of, distribution of and/or use of pornography damages the individual, causing them to enter into mortal sin, a total turning away from God. I don't blame anyone for my addiction. It wasn't necessarily my parent's fault. It wasn't the premium movie channel executive's fault. It was simply the case that a young boy was exposed to disordered sex and inappropriate sexual behavior. Yes, parents must protect their kids, and those who make porn available, especially to children, should be held accountable.

However, please understand that pornography is, in my opinion, the devil's number one tactic in our lifetime to lure men's souls into a life of sin; he tricks us into believing his lies which, like the first lie in the garden, separate us from God and God's love. The devil uses these lies to ruin our souls, and it prevents us from being the men God created us to be. When a man uses porn, who he was created to be is distorted and clouded. Please also understand that porn is a life issue, just like abortion, because porn is fundamentally opposed to life and fails to uphold the dignity of the human person. Is it any wonder that the devil uses his "porn tactics" to kill us and those around us? It shouldn't surprise us... he is after our souls! The social issues of abortion, contraception, same-sex unions, and the proliferation of pornography in our culture are all closely related. Not only are they life issues, they are man-issues. Men cannot sit idly by on the sidelines of these issues any longer. Porn and its acceptance is a major factor in the culture of death. For any parents reading this chapter, please don't assume your kids aren't looking at, watching, using, distributing, streaming, buying, discussing, and experimenting with, emailing, and/or texting/sexting porn. Don't make that assumption! Get into their media, including their mobile media... basically anything that has access to the web or a signal, and put a stop to it. It can and will destroy their lives. The average age children are exposed to porn is now sub-10 years old! That's the average age, not the youngest age. Get filters, accountability software, blocks, time-regulators, and utilize it on ALL of the media devices in your home.

More importantly, talk to your children about this problem openly, discussing the evil, the problems, the addictive nature, and talk to them now! Since I was exposed to this sin at such an early age, I never really knew exactly what I was doing or that it was wrong. I was poorly catechized as a kid and wasn't taught about sexuality and how it played a role in my life. It was only into my mid-teen years that I heard about chastity, virginity, and purity, but by that time, it was too late and my addiction had taken root. When I first realized that I had an addiction to pornography and masturbation, I didn't know what to do. For years, I kept my behavior secretive and never considered telling anyone about it. While some young men experience porn with and around their friends, teammates, or with the neighborhood clan, that was never the case for me. My experience with porn was always secretive and lonely. Finally, in college, I gathered up the courage to go and talk to my best friend and lay it out on the line. I was fed up with my addiction and wanted out badly. "I'm not sure if you have ever" I started, "or if any of the other guys do" I continued. "...but I'm struggling with pornography and masturbation." Wow, what a sense of relief! Even the simple mentioning of these words out loud was empowering. He replied, "Dave, I've struggled for years." "Really? I thought I was the only one!" I had no idea that other men, especially men that I looked up to spiritually and in the ways of the faith, could struggle with something so heinous. I thought I was the only one. After that initial conversation, we entered into an intense and difficult process of accountability, prayer, spiritual direction from priests, and personal self-assessment. It didn't end immediately, but over time, the addiction was overcome. Keep in mind, I didn't say that the temptations went away... they can linger on forever, can change, and can morph into various types of temptations. The hunter continues after us, trying to trip us up, but with the help of God's grace, accountability partners, good strong masculine formation, and a strong will to live chastity, we can attain freedom from sexual sin.

Porn is enticing; it grabs a hold of our senses and is very alluring. The same way that I was lured in as a small boy, porn lures in grown men, too. Porn conquers us because it is self-gratifying. We like visual and physical stimulation, especially sexually. We are wired in a way to be attracted to attractive women and for our bodies to respond to that attraction. Obviously, our culture has successfully skewed what is natural (ie: marital sexual intimacy) into something immoral. The attraction we experience to the opposite sex is natural. This is a good thing, but only when structured in the context of the meaning of man and wife and marital relations. Porn destroys our brain's ability to function properly.

When porn is viewed or used, a chemical bond is created. Many hormones, such as testosterone, are released during sexual activity, while one hormone in particular is specifically damaging in regards to porn use. This chemical is a hormone called oxytocin. Since I'm not a clinician, nor a medical professional, I'll make only a quick reference about oxytocin. Oxytocin exists in both males and females. One of the most commonly known occurrences of the release and effects of oxytocin is in childbirth. It is one of the bonding agents between a mother and a newborn child – a very powerful bond. Forming an intense bond is obviously its intended effect. Oxytocin is also released in sexual orgasm, thus creating an intense bond between those engaged in sexual activity – intended to bond a married couple. When the bond is based on a fantasy and unreality (porn) the bond is incredibly detrimental – bonding the user to falsehood. This false bond distorts the true understanding of the sexual act.

Once the distorted bond is in place, often times, the bond grows more and more distorted. Many men choose to allow this bond into their life and then wonder why real intimacy and actual giving of oneself, especially in marriage, is so difficult. If you haven't been exposed to porn, I urge you to do everything in your power to stay away from it. Porn can be like methamphetamines; it only takes one use and you can become hooked. If you have been exposed to porn, it will continue to bond you to the fantasy, to the sexual act, to the addiction, and making it harder and harder to break free. If you're a single man using porn, the distorted bond will damage your relationships (now and in the future), it will be a stumbling block to finding the right spouse, or possibly any spouse at all. Porn will become your motivation in life. If/when a man is married, porn use can cause him to be selfish in regards to intimacy with his wife, not to mention in day-to-day activities and interactions.

Much of my tendency toward selfishness stems, I believe, from my past pornography use. It made everything I did about me and only me. I completely failed at being the man God created me to be because I was too busy being selfish. This is only one side effect of porn use in my life. If you're a married man using porn, I'm almost 100% certain that in one way or another, the intimacy with your wife is distorted by your addiction. Not only does it distort your relationship with your wife, it distorts the relationship you have with your children, friends, and co-workers. I speak about these troubled relationships, motivations, struggles, and temptations because I had them in my life and I know how hard it can be to deal with. It takes loads of hard work to get over them, as well as daily prayer, the Sacraments and God's grace. Porn hunts for us. It's not like in the past when a man had to be gutsy enough to walk into an 'adult store' and purchase a magazine or VHS over the counter. In those times, the men who frequented those establishments were considered 'pervs' and 'dirty old men' – most guys didn't want to go that direction. In current times, porn is accessible in places we can't even imagine; porn is everywhere.

Porn doesn't wait for us to find it; it comes after us and doesn't stop to knock. Porn charges through the door and welcomes itself into our homes. Over the years, in dealing with my addiction to pornography, I've realized some pretty profound things; things about me, about addiction, the pornography industry, and how to overcome this incredible evil. I liken this sin to a battle, an incredible fight that we enter into against evil. A man must enter into this fight aggressively in order to come out victorious. He cannot be timid and he cannot fight an addiction to porn (or any addiction) because he fears it – the fear of being caught watching porn, the fear of ruining a relationship, the fear of having to confess the same sins (again and again), the fear of his work finding inappropriate material on their computer, the fear of failing, the fear of giving into the temptation, etc. Once it has a grip, it isn't likely to let go, until the prey decides to fight back. This fighting back can't be weak. It must be aggressive, calculated, planned, and executed perfectly in order for the battle to be won. A soldier doesn't go into battle fearful – he goes in confident in his training, his abilities, and his leadership. He knows that because of the work he has invested in (ie: his training), he will prevail. He trusts his leadership to guide him through this tough time, quite possibly the hardest thing he's ever done, or ever will do. This is what soldiers do, and we're the same as the real-life soldiers, except in our situation, our eternal salvation is on the line. Fight aggressively, fight with honor, fight for your life. Go into this battle knowing that you have God on your side, that you can accomplish all things through Him (Philippians 4:13) and that YOU WILL BE VICTORIOUS! So I ask you: are you fighting? Are you ready for battle? Have you been training? When temptations come your way, are you ready for war? Sometimes our sexual battle is only one issue, maybe simply overcoming the urge to masturbate. Sometimes it's a combination of things, such as masturbation along with pornography use. It might also be a combination of multiple things, such as masturbation, pornography, sexual experimentation, drinking, and depression. For me, it never involved drinking, depression, or sadness. It was something that was behind closed doors and hidden from anyone else. It was secretive and seductive. Whatever your situation is, don't kid yourself. Stop justifying your sinful actions. You can achieve freedom from pornography and masturbation.

Believe it: the pornography industry is a giant, preying on unsuspecting victims. I was held captive by a death grip, a grip that left marks, wounds, and scars. For years, I was helpless against pornography's suffocating strikes. I did not know where to turn, or how to start fighting. Thanks to my brothers-in-Christ who helped me along the way, I was able to begin fighting back and eventually, through God's mercy, forgiveness, and strength, I overcame and applied a strangle-hold back upon my aggressor. I'm a big man. I weigh in the mid-200's and stand around six feet tall. I lift (heavy) weights. I workout. I own firearms, bows, knives, and other weapons. I'm proud that I can defend myself and my family from physical attacks. Fights and physicality don't scare me. Okay, big deal... what about it? No matter how big and bad I might be, I am powerless to this sin if I try to go it alone. No amount of weapons, muscles, or fighting skills will make the difference. Alone, we are no match for this giant sin of pornography. If we think that we are tough and capable, and that we can conquer this sin on our own, we are foolish. It is nearly impossible to conquer an addiction without the help of someone else. Later in the chapter I will recommend some steps to conquering this sin but especially, I recommend having an accountability partner: someone to hold you to your commitments, to build you up and encourage you, and someone to help you back up if you should stumble and fall. Pornography and masturbation are mortal sins, meaning that they cut off the life of grace from God the Father. These grave evils will ruin your life, and every single relationship you have in the future.

Don't wait; stand up and fight. Another day gone by without training and without a battle plan is another day you will be held in slavery to the grave evils of pornography and masturbation. Your accountability partner should be battle-planning with you, training with you, and praying right alongside you. Men, whether you've been on the battlefield for a long time or have just begun the fight, I want to encourage you to continue to fight! The devil is strategic in how he attacks you. A period of freedom (any amount of time) can play tricks with a man's mind, giving him a false sense of accomplishment and complacency. No matter how long you've experienced freedom (1 day, 1 month, or 10 years), you must never let your guard down. I'm often asked how long it has been since I've looked at pornography. My answer remains the same: "I didn't look at it today." If I look only towards the past, I will see sin and darkness and will fail to remember that truth and light are ahead of me. I firmly believe that I am, and always will be, in recovery from my addiction; the temptations to fall back into pornography may always be there. I must keep my addiction and more importantly, my recovery, in the right place. If I let down my guard, I am positive that the devil will send a full-on assault against me and try to take me down. The path to holiness is paved by discipline and you must remain disciplined in order to successfully achieve holiness. Holiness, a complete imitation of Christ, is our goal and eternal rest in Heaven is the prize. "There's a way out" If you are currently in porn's grasp, there are ways out.

To get out of your addiction, to overcome, and to experience healing, you will need to pray for and develop, through practice and God's free-gift of grace, virtue. Think of virtues like your muscles. We work our muscles out so that they can perform when needed. Virtue is the same way. You practice, work on the virtue, and then, when the time comes, the virtue is there and ready. Regarding pornography use, you'll want to work on a number of virtues, including chastity, fortitude, and temperance, just to name a few. Possessing the virtue of chastity means that your sexual actions are directed towards the good, the way they were intended by God. This means that your sexual actions, thoughts, and behaviors are in the right context. (I highly recommend reading and studying Pope John Paul II's writings entitled *Love and Responsibility* and *Theology of the Body* to gain much more on this topic.) No matter what you are called to in life, whether you are single, married, a religious priest or brother, all people are called to live chastity, yet our culture tells us something vastly different. When chastity is lived out, it is freeing and from that freedom comes the ability to truly give and to love. Temperance moderates our attraction to pleasure. This can be any form of pleasure... physical, emotional, sexual, mental, etc. There is an opposing vice that we should stay away from... insensibility (the complete rejection of any pleasure). Pleasure, in and of itself, is not bad, as long as it is properly ordered and moderated.

MAN UP! CONTRIBUTORS

DAVE DINUZZO

JARED ZIMMERER

Those Who Came Before Us

MAN UP! CONTRIBUTORS

St. Joseph by Shane Kapler

May 19ᵗʰ – Solemnity of St. Joseph, Spouse of the Blessed Virgin Mary
May 1ˢᵗ – Memorial of St. Joseph the Worker

In any discussion of male saints, Joseph has to head the list. Whether we are single, husbands, fathers, religious brothers, priests, young or old, we can all model ourselves on Joseph. Scripture calls him a "just" man (Mt.1:19). As run-of-the-mill as that might sound in our culture, in the biblical world it was anything but. The same Greek word used to describe Joseph is translated elsewhere in Scripture as "righteous," "upright," and used to describe giants of faith such as King David (1 Sam. 24:17).[28] Joseph was a man of such incredibly deep love and faith that God entrusted to him the two most precious people in the universe – Jesus and Mary.

God prepared Joseph for his vocation from childhood. Unlike Jesus and Mary, Joseph inherited original sin and its effects; so he probably experienced at least some setbacks in learning to say "yes" to God. But Joseph persevered so that by the time we meet him in the gospels he was a man committed to living God's will with all his mind, heart, and strength. What an encouragement to us! God's grace enabled a man, *exactly like you and me*, to become a worthy conduit of both God's husbandly love for the soul of Mary and fatherly love for Jesus. God the Son called Joseph, *"abba,"* father! Think of the patience, perseverance, and greatness of soul Joseph had to exhibit to be placed in that role of imaging God the Father within the Holy Family. Christian husbands and fathers are called to do the same.

It seems natural for us to think that living in friendship with God means that he will direct our path away from hardship and suffering, but St. Joseph's life is proof that it is often just the opposite. Consider the situations that God was either directly responsible for, or permitted to befall Joseph:

- Joseph's new bride was "found to be with child of the Holy Spirit." Joseph was so overwhelmed that he decided to divorce Mary (Mt.1:18-19).
- When it came time for Mary to give birth, the best shelter Joseph could procure for her and the Child was a stable

---

[28] Toschi, Larry M., *Joseph in the New Testament* (Santa Cruz: Guardian of the Redeemer Books, 1991).

- He and his family became fugitives and lived as immigrants in Egypt
- His twelve year old Son disappeared for three days

Any one of those would be enough trouble for most lifetimes but Joseph endured them all, and did so while providing for a family in "third world" conditions. He was a manual laborer, living by the sweat of his brow and beholden to the demands of his customers. Unlike you and me though, Joseph never seemed surprised by any of it. He knew Scripture and understood that it was God's way of molding him: "My child, if you come to serve the Lord, prepare yourself for testing … Accept whatever happens to you, and be patient when you suffer humiliation, because gold is tested with fire, and acceptable people are tested in the furnace of humiliation. Trust him, and he will help you" (Sir.2:1-6).

In good times and bad, Joseph renewed his soul through prayer. He made pilgrimage to the Temple and stayed united to its sacrifices through participation in the synagogue and three times of daily prayer. When God spoke to him, whether it was through Scripture or an angel in a dream, Joseph obeyed immediately. He brought his God-given reason to bear on what he was told too (Mt.2:19-23). In addition, Joseph contemplated Jesus, God-With-Us, in his home. He shared Mary's heart and came to see and understand Jesus through her piercing eyes. (You could say that Joseph was the first soul consecrated to Jesus through Mary.) He shared all of life's activities with Jesus and Mary, and most probably took his last breath in their arms.

This man, this humble man, of whom Scripture records not a single word, is held up by the Church as a model in every area of life: Protector of the Universal Church, Patron of Husbands and Fathers, of Workers and House Hunters, of the Interior Life and of People in Doubt, Patron of a Happy and Holy Death! When in need of a courageous example and the intercession of a man who has 'been there," we should heed Scripture and, "Go to Joseph!" (Gen.41:55)

St. Thomas More: All-Star Father by Jim Burnham

As a role model for fathers, St. Joseph is the obvious first pick. But for a great *back-up* role model, choose St. Thomas More.

If you've seen the movie, *Man for All Seasons*, you know Thomas More (1478–1535) was martyred by King Henry VIII (1491–1547) for refusing to deny papal primacy and the indissolubility of marriage. If you haven't watched the movie, see it with your family ASAP! It's a portrait in courage of a father who gave his life defending faith and family.

Thomas More was among the most accomplished men of his day. Entering Oxford at age 15, he quickly earned a reputation as a scholar and writer. More was fluent in Latin, Greek, and French and was a talented musician. He became a lawyer and also served as a member of Parliament, sheriff of London, ambassador, knight, speaker of the House of Commons, sub-treasurer to the king, and judge. More was the first laymen to become Lord Chancellor, the highest appointed official in England. He stole hours from his sleep to write nine books on apologetics, defending the Catholic faith against the attacks of Luther and other Protestant Reformers. His collected writings fill over 11,000 pages.

For all his professional activities, More put his faith and family first. He rose early to pray, study, and attend daily Mass. For much of his life, he wore a sharp hair shirt next to his skin. Disregarding convention, More gave his four daughters the same classical education as his son. His eldest, Margaret, astonished scholars with her knowledge of Greek and Latin.

More's home was holy, but never stuffy. At the height of his political career, he moved his family to a 32-acre farm in the English countryside and commuted by boat to London. He filled his house with laughter, merriment, and pets, including birds, foxes, and weasels. His friend, the great scholar Erasmus, described him: "His countenance is in harmony with his character, being always expressive of an amiable joyousness, and even an incipient laughter and, to speak candidly, it is better framed for gladness than for gravity or dignity.... He is full of jokes and banter." For amusement, More kept in-residence both a jester and a mischievous monkey.

But trouble came swiftly. After Henry's wife of many years, Catherine of Aragon, failed to produce a male heir, Henry resolved to divorce her and marry Anne Boleyn. Upholding the Church's teaching, Pope Clement refused to annul their valid marriage. Furious, Henry broke with Rome, proclaimed himself Supreme Head of the Church in England, married Anne, and divorced Catherine.

More resigned as Chancellor and lived on a meager 100 pounds a year. He carefully avoided Anne's coronation in 1533, and any statements about the King's situation. However, in March 1534, the Act of Succession was passed requiring an oath rejecting the Pope's authority and acknowledging the nullity of Henry and Catherine's marriage. True to his Catholic beliefs, More refused. He was jailed and pressured for 15 months to comply. He said nothing beyond declaring himself the King's faithful subject. In July 1535, a mock court—using false testimony—convicted More of treason and sentenced him to death.

More's humor endured to the end. On July 6, as he climbed the rickety scaffold for his beheading, More told his executioner: "I pray you, Mr. Lieutenant, see me safe up, and for my coming down let me shift for myself." As he put his head on the block, More carefully moved his beard out of harm's way, saying it had committed no crime and didn't deserve the ax. His final heroic words: "I die the King's good servant, but God's first."

St. Thomas Aquinas, Portrait of Humility by Doug Bushman

St. Thomas (1225-1274) was born into a family of Italian nobility. He eschewed an assured position of prestige in the well-established Order of St. Benedict in order to become a second-generation disciple in a new and comparatively unproven order founded by St. Dominic. This vocational choice already points to humility as a prominent virtue in St. Thomas' life. Influence and recognition were not motivating values for him. Rather, his only concern was to submit to the will of God in all things, regardless of the implications.

Most people who know something about St. Thomas think first of his remarkable intellectual gifts. But these should be seen in the context of a profound humility. For St. Thomas, the humble man submits to whatever is of God in another, and thereby submits to God himself. In his vocation as a teacher, St. Thomas submitted to the truth wherever he found it, no matter what the source. He also embraced the vow of obedience, and submitted to his religious superiors, and to the Church. His theological and philosophical writings were accomplished in the spirit of humble submission to the duties of his assignments as well as the requests of prelates, popes, and friends. In humility, he received the direction for his life from others, taking them as certain indicators of God's wise plan for him.

An often-overlooked feature of St. Thomas' humility is his submission to the way that God crafted the human mind to think. With a discursive intellect, man can only consider one subject at a time. Recognizing this, St. Thomas humbly moved from one subject to another, ordering all the subjects of his inquiry into an unsurpassed theological synthesis.

St. Thomas is a model for all men of the humility that dispels pride, making it possible for a man to take his place in God's plan. If there are indicators of his own will, these are found in the seriousness with which he took the pursuit of truth and the refutation of error. Otherwise, his personality is to be self-effacing before the truth, which he regarded as greater than himself. He was, then, a servant of God, of the truth, of the Church, and of all mankind.

Humility is the foundation of a man's strength because the humble man recognizes that he has no strength of his own: "The Lord is my strength" (Ex 15:2; Is 12:2; Jer 16:19). St. Paul put it this way: "for when I am weak, then I am strong" (2 Cor 10:3).

In his primary vocation as a religious and his vows of poverty, chastity, and obedience, St. Thomas prods all men to be mindful that the world around us "is passing away" (1 Cor 7:31), and thus that the definitive fulfillment of their manhood consists in the perfection of charity and striving for heaven. Because relationships last – relationships with God, family, and friends – men need to learn to measure their fulfillment in terms of these relationships. In his vocation as a theologian, St. Thomas reminds men that fidelity to the truth, especially in acts of conscience, constitutes the true dignity of a man. Finally, his humility teaches us that true virility and masculine strength is fundamentally an interior reality. It is the full development of all the Christian virtues, and this is the Christian man's way to leave a positive mark on history, serving the Church in the humility that is prompt to accede to every indication of God's will.

St Peter (died 64 A.D.) by Jesse Romero

A native of Bethsaida, a village near lake Tiberius, he was the son of John. He was called Simon, and lived and worked as a fisherman on Lake Genesareth. His brother Andrew introduced him to Jesus, who gave him the name 'Cephas,' the Aramaic equivalent of the Greek Peter (the Rock). He was present at Christ first miracle at Cana and at his home at Caperanaum when Jesus cured his mother in law, and his boat was always available to the Savior. When Peter acknowledged Jesus as "the Christ. . . the son of the living God" (Matt 16: 16), the Lord replied, "You are Peter and on this rock I will build my Church" (Matt 16: 18) and "I will give you the keys to the kingdom of heaven: Whatever you bind on earth will be bound in heaven; whatever you loose on earth, will be loosed in heaven." These statements underlay Catholic teaching that Peter was the first Pope and the whole Catholic concept of the primacy of the papacy. Peter is mentioned more frequently than any of the other apostles, he was with Jesus during many of his miracles, but denied him in the courtyard of Pontius Pilate's palace, where Jesus was being held prisoner.

He was the head of the Christians after the Ascension, he designated Judas successor, he was the first to preach to the Gentiles, he was the first apostle to perform a miracle and converted many with his preaching. He was imprisoned by Herod Agrippa in about 43 A.D., but guided by an angel, escaped and firmly proclaimed that Christ wanted the Good News preached to all at the assemble in Jerusalem. After this episode he is not mentioned in the NT again, but a very early tradition says he went to Rome, where he was Rome's first bishop and was crucified there at the foot of Vatican Hill in about 64 A.D. during the reign of Emperor Nero. Eusebius states: In the second year of the two hundredth and fifth Olympiad [A.D. 42]: The Apostle Peter, after he has established the church in Antioch, is sent to Rome, where he remains as a bishop of that city, preaching the gospel for twenty five years (The Chronicle-303 A.D).

Kepha (Aramaic for Rock)
Cephas (transliteration of Kepha in Greek).
Petra or **Petros** (Greek for Rock) [Gerhard Kittel's theological dictionary of the New Testament; vol 6, p.108].

The *Quo Vadis* story is one of those legends of the Saints that are well-known to Catholics but practically unknown to Protestants. It is an ancient legend concerning Peter's martyrdom, believed to be from the second century, and preserved in the collection of legends included in the apocryphal *Acts of Peter*. George Edmundson in *The Church in Rome in the First Century* (London, 1913) summarizes the legend thus: His friends, so runs the story, had entreated the Apostle to save his life by leaving the city. Peter at last consented, but on condition that he should go away alone. But when he wished to pass the gate of the city, he saw Christ meeting him. Falling down in adoration he says to Him 'Lord, whither goest Thou?' [Latin, *quo vadis?*] And Christ replied to him 'I am coming to Rome to be again crucified.' And Peter says to Him 'Lord, wilt Thou again be crucified?' And the Lord said to him 'Even so, I will again be crucified.' Peter said to Him 'Lord, I will return and will follow Thee.' And with these words the Lord ascended into Heaven . . . And Peter, afterwards coming to himself, understood that it was of his own passion that it had been spoken, because that in it the Lord would suffer. The Apostle then returned with joy to meet the death which the Lord had signified that he should die.

St. Josemaria Escriva by Kevin Lowry

St. Josemaria Escriva was born in Spain in 1902. He was born into a devout Catholic family and sensed a calling to the priesthood early in his life. He studied law before his ordination in 1925, and it didn't take long afterwards for the Lord to call St. Josemaria to found Opus Dei (meaning "work of God") in 1928. He went on to obtain doctorates in law and theology, but he is perhaps best remembered for Opus Dei, often referred to informally as "the work."

Contrary to popular novels, Opus Dei is not a secretive society – it's a personal prelature of the Catholic Church (its website is www.opusdei.org). Members are faithful to the Holy Father and include priests, associates, consecrated singles ("numeraries") and married men and women ("supernumeraries"). The spirituality of Opus Dei is one of complete dedication to personal sanctity, particularly in one's work and the ordinary circumstances of daily life.

Perhaps more than any other contemporary organization within the Church, Opus Dei strives to encourage holiness in ordinary daily activities, particularly work. In fact, St. Josemaria was active behind the scenes during Vatican II advocating this position, considered radical by many within the Church. However, the notion that everyone can – and should – strive for sanctity regardless of their state in life has since flourished.

St. Josemaria Escriva exemplified the life he encouraged, working, preaching, and writing tirelessly for decades until his death in 1975. On October 6, 2002, Bl. John Paul II canonized St. Josemaria in an event attended by thousands, including Opus Dei members from around the world.

Today, Opus Dei has almost 90,000 members around the world and offers spiritual formation through classes, retreats, and spiritual direction. St. Josemaria's emphasis on divine filiation, prayer, sacrifice and sanctifying our daily work continues to resonate through the lives of countless people touched by his work around the world.

Father Vincent Capodanno
"The Grunt Padre"—servant of God by Dave DiNuzzo Sr.

Vincent Capodanno was born on February 13, 1929 to an Italian-Catholic family living on Staten Island, New York. Vincent joined the Maryknoll Missionaries at the age of 20, and was sent to Taiwan on his first assignment out of seminary to serve in an Taiwanese parish and school. He also worked at a school in Hong Kong. After these first two assignments with the Maryknolls, Fr. Vincent requested the ability to become a chaplain in the United States Navy.

After his time in office candidate school, Fr. Vincent was assigned to the 7th Marines, and in 1966, deployed to Vietnam. It was said of Fr. Vincent that he gained the reputation of "always being there – for always taking care of his Marines."

In 1967, while deployed to Vietnam, Fr. Vincent learned of a battle that had started between a drastically outnumbered 5th Marines battalion and over 2,500 North Vietnamese troops. He sat in on briefings and after gathering information, requested to go to the battlefield.

When in place, the fighting became extreme and intense. They had horrible conditions in the deep jungle of Vietnam. He requested to be on the front lines, with the soldiers who were part of the most dangerous of fighting. He was there to minister to them, give them last rites should they need them, and ultimately, to be present to his Marines who needed him.

Fr. Vincent was himself wounded after an enemy explosive detonated nearby. Part of his face and the majority of his right hand were wounded significantly, but despite these injuries, he continued to serve the troops. He refused aid, and responded to the call of a wounded medic, in an exposed location. He shielded him with his body, saying "Stay quiet, Marine. God is with us all this day." While trying to defend his fellow Marine, Fr. Vincent was shot multiple times by enemy machine guns, dying on the battlefield. He gave the ultimate sacrifice; he laid down his life in service to the Lord. He received both the Bronze Star and the Medal of Honor after his death. Imagine how hard it must have been for him to enter into an intense battle like the one that was going on that day. Yet, he trusted in the Lord and was willing to give up his life.

Men can take a great deal from the story of Fr. Vincent. He was a servant leader, and desired to serve God in all that he did. He lived heroic virtue. Fr. Vincent heard the call to the priesthood at a young age and followed that call, ultimately to his death. It most certainly wasn't an easy task, but he did the seemingly impossible task, and his reward is in Heaven. Because Fr. Vincent lived recently, many people who knew him are still living, a great reminder that holiness and sainthood are not out of our reach in this day and age.

Fr. Vincent was officially named "Servant of God" in 2006, starting the process of his canonization to sainthood.

Blessed Junipero Serra by Marlon De La Torre

"All my life I have wanted to be a missionary. I have wanted to carry the gospel message to those who have never heard of God and the Kingdom he has prepared for them."

Blessed Junipero Serra desired to save souls. He was a man who possessed a desire to serve others at his own spiritual and physical expense. In many ways he exemplifies what it it means to be a man of God, a soldier for Christ in the Twenty-first century.

A native of Majorca, Spain, Blessed Serra was born on Friday, November 24, 1713. He was the third of five children, baptized on the day of his birth and given the baptismal name of Miguel Jose Serra. Upon his ordination he took the name Junipero meaning "Jester of God." Known to be a brilliant student, he excelled in his studies especially philosophy earning his doctorate and becoming Chair of Philosophy at the University of Palma for his Franciscan order in 1749. In this same year he volunteered to become a missionary to the new world traveling to Mexico and then onto the California territories to evangelize and convert the native tribes. Before his departure he leaves his students with one final message: I desire nothing more from you that this that when the news of my death shall have reached your ears, I ask that you say for the benefit if my soul 'May he rest in peace, and I shall not fail to do the same for you so that all of us will attain that goal for which we have been created. Amen and farewell . . . I am no longer your professor, but your most humble servant." (Diary of Junipero Serra, p. 15)

Determined to foster conversion wherever he went Fr. Serra systematically established twenty-one missions up the California coast walking over twenty-four thousand miles while converting thousands of Indians and catechizing them via a translation of the catechism into the local Indian languages of the time.

His model of holiness is a trait all men should aspire to. His travels began beyond his middle-age years when most men would not think of engaging in such work. He traveled with two physically debilitating ailments, asthma and an ulcerated leg which was with him for over fifteen years. Blessed Serra was determined to bring the Gospel to all of God's children at the expense of his own health. His witness was a form of self-mortification for the souls he would encounter revealing an apostolic zeal few could match. One endearing trait was his intense devotion to the Blessed Mother calling upon her intercessory prayers throughout his travels.

Blessed Serra stressed the need to centralize all activity to Christ in the Holy Eucharist hence the establishment of the twenty-one missions to celebrate the Holy Sacrifice of the Mass. His absolute confidence in God served him well in establishing the Missions and evangelizing California. He continued his godly mission until his body could bear no more dying at the age of 70 from tuberculosis.

Blessed Junipero Serra wrote a final farewell to his parents prior to his new missionary journey to the new world. His words resonate to all of us today as a call of duty to serve the Church: ". . . always encourage me to go forward, and never turn back . . . Let them rejoice that they have a son who is a priest, though an unworthy one and a sinner, . . . In order to become a good religious I have set out on this course . . . Blessed be God. May His holy will be done."(Diary of Fr. Junipero Serra p. 15)

St. Albert of Cologne: Great Man and Great Saint by Kevin Vost

"The great man is often petty in the eyes of those who are nearest to him and who see the weakness of his character. There is a proverb which says that no man is a hero to his valet de chambre. But the saint is holiest of all in the eyes of those who live with him and who are witnesses of his hidden virtues, his tenderness of heart, his power with God, and his secret influence over souls." Henri Joly, The Psychology of the Saints

"Albertus Magnus" – Albert the Great. Is that a manly name or what? St. Albert the Great (c.1200 – 1280 AD), one of the handful of people we revere within the Church with the moniker "the Great," was one of those even rarer souls who were known as "the Great," even while alive. St. Albert was called great because of his peerless breadth of knowledge. He contributed to virtually every science of his day from "a" to "z," -- from anatomy, anthropology, astronomy, biology, botany, chemistry, dentistry, geography, geology, medicine, physiology, physics, and psychology -- all the way to zoology. And this is not to mention his mastery of philosophy, Scripture, and theology as well, Albert being so aware that all of creation speaks in some way of its Creator. Some have even called St. Albert the last man who knew all there was to know! I think then that we can safely say that St. Albert had manned up his mind.

St. Albert was also more than just a mind, even a very great one. He was a great man. A truly masculine man lifts up those who are under his care, and is delighted when those he has formed rise even higher than he. His own most towering student, (perhaps you've heard of him – St. Thomas Aquinas), died six years before Albert. When some theologians attacked Thomas's teachings after his death, the aging Albert made time to read his student's Summa Theologica. Albert happily acknowledged its superiority to his own work and proceeded to boldly speak out and champion Thomas's thought. Some call him "the first Thomist." While St. Thomas would be canonized in 1323, less than 50 years after his death, his great, though humble teacher would await another six hundred years, being declared a saint and Doctor of the Church only in 1931. (I doubt that he minded the wait.)

St. Albert was also a true "Renaissance Man" well before the "Renaissance." He was not only a "thinker," but a "doer" as well. Dominicans seek to share with others the fruits of their contemplation, and Albert produced a most abundant harvest across all of Europe throughout his long life. Not only did he share his encyclopedic knowledge as a professor at the University of Paris and in Dominican houses of study, he also served as the German provincial of Order of Preachers, as Bishop of Regensburg, as preacher of a crusade, as a pontifical advisor, and as a settler of legal and ecclesiastical disputes.

Though a thinker and a doer, St. Albert knew well that charity is the highest of virtues, and he was a remarkable "lover" as well. St. Albert loved Christ and His mother, writing profoundly on the Eucharist and beautifully on the Virgin Mary. Some say he was the most prolific Mariologist of his time. His manly heart went out as well to the women in his life. St. Albert was a beloved confessor and great benefactor of many convents of Dominican and other religious sisters.

In short, St. Albert the Great was a great man and a great saint because he used all his great gifts for the glory of God and in the service of the men and women of his day. Though a thinker by nature, he always heeded the call when God called bid him go forth from the ivory tower of the study into the streets of the world that so badly needed his guidance. Perhaps St. Albert's great lesson to us lesser men is to tirelessly seek to develop whatever gifts God has given us, so that with them we might help raise up toward heaven our brothers and sisters, and sons and daughters in Christ.

St. Antony of the Desert by Fr. Steve Grunow

"From the days of John the Baptist until now, the kingdom of heaven suffers violence, and the violent bear it away..."

The Church is a revolutionary movement. I know rhetoric like that makes people nervous, but there is no way around accepting this as Christ's will for the Church if you are in any way going to take his revelation seriously. As a point of reference, consider the alarming "Magnificat" of Christ's Holy Mother, in which she testifies to what amounts to the world being turned upside down with the mighty cast down and the lowly lifted up, the hungry filled up and the rich sent away empty. For a couple decades the Church convulsed itself in an internal argument as to what kind of social theory Christ's revelation intended to impart. For some, it seemed that Christ came to give divine sanction to the violent overthrow of the political and economic status quo and his authority could be invoked to justify totalitarian systems. Not so! Said the Church. Yes, there is a revolution, but it is not like the revolutions that the powers of the world use to accomplish and justify their will to dominate.

Instead, the revolution of the Church is the coming of God's kingdom into the world through profound risks of faith, hope and charity, theological virtues that bear themselves into the lives of Christ's disciples and effect a transformation that can seem as violent as a revolution. It is from those virtues that the subversive forces of poverty, chastity and obedience emerge. Those subversive forces, called the evangelical counsels, are not imposed on Christ's disciples, but accepted as the way of life the Lord Jesus has intended to emerge from an acceptance of the theological virtues in their most radical form. The way of life that is the evangelical counsels is the Church's revolution, transforming not only the disciple, but also the culture in which the disciple is sent as a missionary of Christ's Kingdom. The testimony of this missionary is not simply words, but it is embodied in a their very person. The missionary does not just proclaim faith, hope and charity. The missionary looks like faith, hope and charity and will most look like these theological virtues in their practice of poverty, chastity and obedience.

It is correct to see John the Baptist as the forerunner of this revolution for embodied in his witness is the thick descriptions of the theological virtues and the practices of the evangelical counsels. Thus, does the Lord Jesus refer to John the Baptist as one in whom the "Kingdom of Heaven suffers violence" by which is meant the revolutionary transformation of the exemplified by the Baptist where all that he has is surrendered in service of a Kingdom that will overcome the world through radical acts of faith, hope and charity. This radical commitment will inevitably be received by the body of the witness and the culture in which the witness is embedded as violence, for the poverty, chastity and obedience which are the radicalized expressions of faith, hope and love, will undermine and seek to overturn what is contrary to their way of life. This is the Church's revolution.

John the Baptist was not without heirs. Saint Anthony of the Desert was born in the year 251 AD, the son of wealthy landowners in the region of Herakleopolic Magna, a territory within the lands of ancient and mysterious Egypt. As a young man, the revolutionary proclamation of the Kingdom of God in Christ as expressed in the 19th chapter of the Gospel of Matthew provoked in him profound wonder: "If you wish to be perfect, go and sell what you have and give it to the poor and you will have treasure in heaven. Then come follow me." And so he did. After the death of his parents, he made the necessary arrangements for care for his sister, and then applied the words of Christ literally- he sold what he had and followed Christ. This following of Christ opened up for Athanasius a path that led out in the wilderness of the Nitriandesert, and into places that men like John the Baptist choose as their homes. In the desert, life is directed first and foremost by immediate need and necessity and worldly pre-occupations of life fall away if one's life is to be preserved. The desert is a crucible in which preoccupation with the satisfaction of desire yields to attainment of only what is truly necessary. In this way and on this path, Anthony stripped himself of his not only his possessions, but also the illusion that what comforts he had known were what were necessary.

The crucible of the desert presented physical challenges that temper a man's character like steel, but also provoke the soul of a man to contend with all that is within him that resists Christ and prefers one's own will to his. Anthony found himself beset by spiritual powers which were manifestations of the noon day devil which tempts us to acedia, or the boredom and laziness that subvert our desire to do the necessary interior work so that we might better embody and practice the theological virtues. Like a man of our own time, this acedia often afflicted him with a desire for pornographic fantasies. But the saint resisted, and in his resistance those temptations revealed themselves to be nothing more than illusions that "disappeared like smoke." Once Anthony accepted the illusionary nature of his desires for wealth, pleasure, power and honor, these things lost their ability to entice and to control. Anthony became a free man and he was free, not for himself, but for the mission that the Lord gave him.

And what was that mission? It was to inspire a revolutionary movement.

Saint Anthony's path led him out of his culture, one like our own culture, and one that defines a man by how he has fulfilled his desires for wealth, pleasure, power and honor. Yet the retreat from one culture was to lead him to another culture, one that would better embody the revolutionary nature of the Church and the radicalized way of life that is engendered from the theological virtues. Anthony's new culture happens in his formation of a new community of disciples who would embody a new cultural form by living in accord with poverty, chastity and obedience. This new cultural form lays siege to the foundations of cultures that have established themselves as kingdoms contrary to the Kingdom of God in Christ.

Anthony made a counter-intuitive move as a missionary disciple. Instead of embedding himself within the culture, he removed himself from it, and in did so to indicate that an alternative way of life existed that intended to change that culture. His intentional withdrawal would engender fascination and this fascination would draw others from their status quos into something that would strike them as a surprise- and the surprise was that there existed in Christ's way of life another way of life than what they knew. There in the desert, living waters of grace would nourish the seeds from which the great trees of what the Church now calls monastic and consecrated life would flourish and grow.

Monastic and consecrated life is not intended as retreats from reality or quiet places of withdrawal from the world. Monastic and consecrated life are established as a counter-cultural witness to a world (and the Church) that forgets that the revelation of Christ in faith, hope and charity demands that the kingdoms of the world give way to the kingdom of Christ. Rather than places of peace, the monastery, the convent, the hermitage is a place of violence, where the Kingdom of Heaven is seized by the force of faith, hope and love by saints like Anthony of the Desert.

Blessed Pier Giorgio Frassati: The Man of the Beatitudes by Jared Zimmerer

In learning about what it means to be a true Catholic renaissance man of today, Blessed Pier Giorgio Frassati is the culmination of everything you have read. He was well versed in the poems of Dante. He had an immense appreciation of theatre and the opera. He could climb peaks with the best of them while reciting scripture and singing praises of the beauty of the mountains. He smoked tobacco from a pipe and was a known prankster. He dutifully fought communism and fascism. He fed the poor and visited the sick. He knew his Catholic faith inside and out and received the Eucharist almost daily. Pier Giorgio was handsome, athletic, compassionate, humble, intelligent, authentic, and joyful. Undeniably, he enveloped all things manly.

Pier Giorgio Frassati was born in Turin, Italy on April 6th, 1901. He was born into an affluent family, his mother an artist and his father the owner of the newspaper *La Stampa* and an influential politician. At an early age Pier Giorgio had a love for the poor often bringing his weekly allowance to the poor even at the young age of 6. Pier Giorgio's father, Alfredo, an agnostic himself, allowed Pier Giorgio to be taught in the faith by the Jesuits and Salesians, though in the home Pier Giorgio was largely self-taught through his love of prayer and tradition. Pier Giorgio was a passionate young man who did not allow his family's status effect the way he treated others or how others treated him.

Once as a young boy his father neglected to give a poor man any food and Pier Giorgio ran to his mother in tears screaming, "Mama, there was a poor, hungry man at the door and Papa did not give him anything to eat!" Unable to calm Pier Giorgio down, his mother sent for the poor man to come back to the home for something to eat and drink. Later when finding out that the man had lied about his need the young Pier Giorgio replied, "But what if it was Jesus who sent us that poor man?" His love of the poor extended throughout his entire life. On his death bed, he wrote a note to his friend to be sure that the medicines he was bringing to a sick person made it and where it must go.

His life was full of great joy and sorrows, which were often felt to the utmost because Pier Giorgio was a man of the heart. He was not afraid of his passions but rather through his masculinity knew when and where they ought to be expressed. At seventeen years old he joined the Marian Sodality, the St. Vincent Society, the confraternity of the Rosary and the Italian Alpine club, all of which encircles his major passions in life. He would often lead his peers to the mountain for a day of skiing or hiking while discussing the Church, politics, or reciting entire lines of Dante's *Divine Comedy* in its original Latin. Unbeknownst to his friends the majority of these days were started at daily mass as early as 4 a.m. for Pier Giorgio. At the age of 21, Pier Giorgio was accepted into the Third Order Lay Dominicans, which came after a few years of discernment and his deep devotion to the rosary.

Pier Giorgio was a staunch anti-fascist and anti-communist. Once at a Church-organized anti-fascist rally in Rome, Pier Giorgio and his friends were leading the way when the authorities came to put it to a stop with violence. After many of his friends were arrested and beaten, Pier Giorgio grabbed their banner, which had been knocked out of a fellow Catholics hands, rallying the other young people to continue peacefully yet zealously. One of the best ways I have heard Pier Giorgio described is that he lived with a wild tranquility. He was an intense person. He loved intensely, he prayed intensely, but he never shied away from the tranquil peace of the solitude in the presence of Christ.

When Pier Giorgio was twenty-one he also joined the FUCI (Italian Catholic University Federation), which had a bulletin board on which it would post its announcements and upcoming events. One day a group of anti-clerical young men approached the board to destroy its postings when Pier Giorgio stood between the board and the men. Later, when the board was destroyed and Pier Giorgio was covered in scrapes he bruises he walked home with his pride and dignity. Pier Giorgio was a man of courage and tenacity which was engrained through his love of the Catholic faith and his people.

Out of his endless passions and pursuits in faith a few in particular stood out: the love of the poor and helpless, the Blessed Sacrament, and devotion to Our Lady; the sacred triad of commitmentfor anyone desiring to become a saint. His love of humanity stretched from the depths of his love of Christ and the Catholic faith. Through culture, athletics, patriotism, and simply living as a gentleman, Pier Giorgio made sanctity within reach for everyone. He allowed his love of the Faith to control his passions and his encounters with others. Pier Giorgio died at the young age of twenty-four on July 4th, 1925 of poliomyelitis, which he undoubtedly contracted from his work with the sick. His body was exhumed in 1981 and found to be completely intact and incorrupt. On May 20th, 1990 Bl. Pope John Paul 2 beatified the man who he said, "I wanted to pay homage to a young man who was able to witness to Christ with singular effectiveness in this century of ours. When I was a young man, I, too, felt the beneficial influence of his example and, as a student, I was impressed by the force of his testimony."

On a picture of himself hanging off the side of a cliff, he once wrote, "Verso L'Alto!" meaning "To the Top!" May we take his message to heart and desire to live to the utmost, fight for those who cannot fight for themselves and reach the heavens by way of prayer and devotion. Pier Giorgio was indeed The Man of the Beatitudes who the New Catholic Renaissance Man should desire to emulate. In his ordinary ways he lived extraordinarily.

Saint Benedict by Deacon Harold Burke-Sivers

Saint Benedict was born in Nursia, Italy in the year 480 AD and is most famous for his *Rule for Monks*, which is to this day the most common and influential Rule for monasteries and monks in the world. Benedict had such a profound influence on the development of European civilization and culture that among the titles given to him by the Church are "Founder of Western Monasticism" and "Patron Saint of Europe."

Saint Benedict speaks to his monks like a father speaks to his sons, imbuing the Benedictine motto of *ora et labora* (pray and work) into their minds and hearts. This should also be the motto of all men who seek deeper union with Christ through an active prayer life and fruitful participation in the redemptive work of Christ through his vocation in the secular world.

Saint Benedict was not a fan of much talking, telling his monks that "the spirit of silence is so important, permission to speak should rarely be granted."[xxiv] He insisted that "monks ought to be zealous for silence at all times"[xxv] so that they could hear God's voice. But how do we "hear" God? In order to truly hear the Lord we must take Saint Benedict's advice: "Listen to the Master's precepts and incline the ear of the heart." [xxvi]

The key to listening with your heart is silence. Following the example of Saint Benedict, we must foster an atmosphere of prayerful silence in order to hear the Word of God and allow that voice to change our lives. Attending Eucharistic Adoration for one hour every week is a great way to accomplish this. The fruits of Eucharistic adoration speak for themselves: stronger devotion to Jesus, a profound desire for repentance and conversion, and a deeper longing for personal holiness.

Saint Benedict states that prayer is an "act of listening, which must then be expressed in action. [...] Thus, the monk's life becomes a fruitful symbiosis between action and contemplation, 'so that God may be glorified in all things.' The first and indispensable commitment of a disciple of Saint Benedict is the sincere search for God on the path mapped out by the humble and obedient Christ, whose love he must put before all else, in the service of the other."[xxvii]

Men must be actively engaged in the secular world as "signs of courage and intellectual creativity in the privileged places of culture: the world of education, in places of scientific and technological research, the areas of artistic creativity, and works in the humanities".[xxviii] By successfully integrating work and prayer, a man orders his life in such a way that "there cannot be two parallel lives in their existence: on the one hand, the so-called spiritual life, with its values and demands, and on the other hand, the so-called secular life, that is, life in a family, at work, in social relationships, in the responsibilities of public life and in culture."[xxix]

My bothers in Christ, Saint Benedict's motto *ora et labora* (pray and work) should serve as the model for a balanced life. Through his intercession, let us clean out the caverns and dark places of our lives so that Jesus may come and make his home with us. Let us get past our preoccupation with the materiality of the culture and allow God's power and peace, God's love and life to draw us into a place where there is nothing standing between us and our ability to become the person He created us to be. Let us pray with Saint Benedict to freely give ourselves over to God's will so completely that we "prefer absolutely nothing to the love of Christ."[xxx]

A Higher Calling On Your Life

DAVE DINUZZO SR.

It is the hope of this book that by reading it, you have been challenged. Reading these various topics written about becoming the new Catholic Renaissance Man, we hope that you take time to look inward at how you are living your call towards authentic masculinity. Hopefully the authors have called you to something higher. To become the new Catholic Renaissance Man is not something to be taken lightly, but a reality check, and a calling towards holiness and virtue. In a world that expects and condones mediocrity from men, it is time for us to show that there are still men of action, men of courage, men of meaning, and men with purpose.

Our culture has sold us a lie, and many of us are consuming this lie at incredible rates. The lie tells us that males are more manly based on how much power, money, sex, and stuff they consume and amass. I call this "cultural manliness." We are told that the more of these "things" we get, the more manly we are and the happier we will become. On the contrary, the more of these things that we consume, the more damaged our masculinity becomes and the further we stray from happiness. Because so many men are buying this lie, our culture is suffering tragically. Cultural manliness demands selfishness, arrogance, and abuse of power and status. These characteristics will continue to force us down a path of self-destruction.

The culture suffers from broken men who fail to lead, to protect, and to provide. Our brothers have no idea what it takes to be a man and they wallow in despair, addiction, pain, and suffering with no answers. They have no purpose, nothing pushing them on. They have failed to see the mission before them, and have given way to apathy. Apathy is killing us; it is destroying our culture. Men sit by, not caring that atrocities are happening, such as the slaughter of millions upon millions of innocent human babies. Not caring about the destruction of the family, of the culture, of our rights and our freedoms.

When apathy takes over, men fail to fulfill their God-given

mission. They fail to see that God has called them, each and every one of them, and that He has great things in store for them. Men spend their lives on the sidelines, cloaked in sin and darkness, completely unaware of what's happening around them. They believe that the struggles and difficulties of the world have nothing to do with them and that the problems of the world are someone else's issue to deal with. These men fail to see that they can effect positive change in the world around them. It is time that we stop living vicariously through action-flick actors, rock stars, and professional athletes and realize that heroism is within us! The natural call of all men, to lead, protect, and provide, is for all men. None are exempt. You cannot sit on the sidelines any longer. You must pick up your weapons and fight. The culture of death will continue to steal souls away for evil if good men don't stand up and fight. It is not acceptable to make excuses. You cannot ride the fence of indifference.

To win in the battle of good versus evil, good men must choose to fight. To win the battle, good men must do the difficult things in life and put themselves out there, making themselves vulnerable and susceptible to danger, harm, and possibly even death. Are you willing to lay down your life for your spouse? For your children? Your family? For Mother Church? For your faith? Are you willing to be martyred? Are you willing to sacrifice your life so as to gain eternal salvation?

If your answers are no, then it is likely that you have bought the lie. Living a selfish life of cowardice and inaction will lose your soul. But it's not too late. You are reading this book; are you ready to enact change in your life?

If you're not living the life you want, only you can make the changes that need to happen so that you don't just let life happen to you, but that you actually live. It takes daily action and determination to live the way that God has called us to live; a life of holiness and virtue.

Others have gone before us in this same battle and have won! They have set the tone and have shown us the way. Great lives of great saints are our benchmark. The difference between us and the saints is that they lived heroic virtue. You have that potential in you as they once did! People love a good leader, someone who steps up and takes the reins. That can be you! Whatever your life situation, whatever your vocation, whatever your occupation, you have it in you and can do it.

There is a great responsibility that every man is given - the responsibility to fight evil. When you decide to start fighting evil, the devil will come after you. Prepare yourself. The other men who are apathetic, who don't care... they are low-hanging fruit. They aren't ready to fight, many of them unaware of the battle raging around them. They are easy souls for the devil. He doesn't have to put any effort into their demise; he has their souls in queue. The men who decide to fight should ready themselves for on-going assaults from the devil. This is not meant to scare you. On the contrary, it is a rally cry, to call like-minded men, ready to do battle, to prepare themselves and to take action.

Stand up and protect truth and goodness, our families, our churches, our communities, the institution of marriage, and most importantly, protect life. We're called to protect those in our care against evil, from harm, from danger, and that includes protecting those in our care from fear and anxiety. Protect holiness and right relationship with God, which is being destroyed by our culture. Protect generations to come.

Start where you are. Start at home. Take the steps that need to be taken to make your home safe, because if our homes aren't safe, nowhere else can be safe. Daily prayer is an essential in this battle. Sacramental grace is essential. Christ already won the battle. Follow Him and be not afraid. The time is now, men. There are no more practices, no more dress rehearsals. This is it. Stand up and fight.

5 Steps to Overcoming an Addiction to Pornography and Masturbation

STEP 1: Admit That You Have a Problem. If you don't know that you have a problem, you'll never know that you need to overcome anything. Admitting that you have an addiction doesn't solve it, but it gets the process started.

STEP 2: Don't Just Want to Fix the Problem, Work to Fix the

Problem. Simply desiring for an addiction to go away will never make it go away. It requires a large amount of work. Take action. By reading this 5 step plan, you are beginning the journey towards freedom, don't stop!

STEP 3: Find a Brother (Accountability Partner) To Meet with Regularly. In order to overcome a pornography addiction, you must have brotherhood and accountability. It is essential in fighting the battle. Going this alone may very likely end in defeat. You must, from the moment you start holding each other accountable, be 100% open and honest with each other. If you cannot be honest, don't waste their time. Find a brother, do it today. This brother can be any man, but it may be best if you are working on similar battles together. Some might disagree, but your wife is not your accountability partner, she is your wife. She can certainly help you in this journey, but in a different way than a brother-in-the-Lord can.

STEP 4: Make a Plan. Having a plan of how to attack your addiction is essential. Do soldiers sit around at home until they get called to deployment? No, they train and train and train, knowing that when they are in battle and are actually faced with kicking that door in and staring the enemy down, they will succeed. They trust their training. Your plan is part of your training, so that when you are faced with the temptations, you are ready to act. Your plan should address your temptations specifically; therefore, your plan is unique to you and your temptations. The essential piece to having a plan is **ACTING ON THE PLAN AT THE VERY FIRST INSTANCE THAT YOU RECOGNIZE A TEMPTATION.** If you act on your plan within the first second of recognizing a temptation, you are most likely to succeed. If you wait an extra second, your chances of putting up a strong fight are greatly decreased. And if you wait a full three seconds to act, you are setting yourself up for failure. You know your temptations, act quickly when tempted, it will save your life. What does a plan look like? A plan, in this case, is simply a method of reacting to sexual temptation. (Again, it must be an immediate reaction!) Some examples of plans (at the first instance of temptation): praying (The Rosary, a specific prayer, a spontaneous prayer, etc.); calling your accountability partner (any day/time); leaving the room, getting away from the computer, magazines, videos, temptation and so on; leaving the house, office, working out, clicking "close" on your web browser, etc. or a combination of some or all of these—or other things. The plan's initial purpose is in direct response to the temptation. The plan should attack the temptation aggressively and allow for a situational mind/body change. If you are tempted by what's on the internet, make your plan in regards to protecting yourself from the internet. If you are tempted by magazines, make your plan in regards to protecting yourself from the magazines. Your plan must fit your temptations.

STEP 5: Pray. Pray regularly and pray hard. In the same way that David went to battle against Goliath, we too must trust that God will bring us through our battle with the giant and make us victorious. Trust in God and know that your prayer time with Him helps you to know Him better, as with any relationship. If we want to succeed in beating an addiction to porn, we must rely on God for help. We cannot do it alone. Along with daily prayer, you must rely on God's grace from the Sacraments, especially frequent Confession and frequent reception of the Most Holy Eucharist. (A regular confessor is encouraged.)

Fortitude is also called courage. Fortitude ensures firmness in difficulty. It is a resolve to resist temptations. The opposite of fortitude is timidity (cowardice); don't be a coward! Courage helps us to persevere in everyday life. Courage moderates our fear and it helps us live for something great in our lives. There are 3 sub-virtues of Fortitude: 1. Magnanimity (defined as "greatness of soul"), 2. Patience, and 3. Perseverance. Isn't it incredible how perfect the solution is?! Fearlessness and Rash-boldness are counterfeit vices, meaning that they may appear to be courageous, but are actually vicious. When a man is fearless, he doesn't give death or evil their due respect. When a man acts out of rash-boldness, he takes on something that he shouldn't. Be careful to protect against these. I urge all men to call this topic by its proper name if you really want to deal with the issue. You'll notice that I previously used the word struggle, to describe my addiction. I did that because it is one of the common terms used to describe the sins related to lust and lack of chastity. Get away from using the term "struggle." Be a man and call your addiction what it is. It is failure. It is sin. If you attempt to water it down and sugar coat it, you won't truly deal with it and it will consume you further.

Calling our porn use out prevents us from sugar coating it. Although it may seem like there will never be freedom from your addiction to pornography, rest assured, and know that there is hope. I'm a walking testimony to the power that the Lord provides a man when he seeks assistance. Freedom awaits you! Freedom, however, does not come cheap. The road ahead will most likely be long and troubled; continue to fight every day. Some men need additional assistance beyond accountability partners and priests to administer the Sacraments, requiring psychotherapy, and possibly even medication.

There are a number of very qualified and successful counselors who can help you in this area. In addition, there are very successful groups throughout the country that help men overcome their sexual addictions. Whatever your need is, be willing to put the effort forth to seek the help and resources that you require.

What I have experienced from living free from porn is hard to describe. My life is no longer controlled by my passions, and I have the ability to live in the light, making it possible to be the husband and father, son and friend, that I always knew I could be. Porn controlled me and held me down, making me a slave. Now that the chains of bondage to this sin are gone, I can truly live.

THE RISE AND FALL OF HONOR
A Short Story of the Modern American Male

JARED ZIMMERER

PHASE 1: COMMENCEMENT OF ORDERS
"The first thing to do when you awake is to open the windows of your soul. Consider yourself as on the field of battle, facing the enemy and bound by the iron-clad law—either fight or die." ~ Lorenzo Scupoli, The Spiritual Combat

On the 8th veil of heaven there resided a recently promoted angel named Zacharael. Known for his angelic wisdom and perseverance, he progressed his way through the orders to the level of Sentinel. To Light, To Guard, To Rule, To Guide (as it says on the breastplate and creed of the Sentinel Angels) he had just received his first assignment: the safeguard of a fresh militant soul. Zachareal had been trained by the great Raphael himself, taught that human souls are very precious to The Commander and therefore Sentinel Angels were to treat each and every soul as if it were the only one worthy of heaven. Raphael had taught him that the battlefield is very real and that unless the young one whom Zachareal was now charged to watch did not take full advantage of the spiritual armor given by the Pillar of Truth, then doom would befall the poor soul. Raphael had thoroughly imparted to Zachareal that the cowardly (sinful) behavior of the militants of Lucifer dominated the physical world; hence the vocation of Sentinels were more vital than ever. For those that wished to serve The Commander, angelic assistance was indispensable.

Raphael now warned and reminded Zachareal of what could befall his squire should Zachareal fail him. "I remember many battles ago against Asmodeus, that monster of the bridal chamber, who tried to ruin a poor young woman, Sarah was her name, but through the intervention of the good and faithful fighter Tobit we were able to help Sarah. You see, young Zachareal, it is to the men that The Commander has charged with the defense of the innocent. So, our job is to guide and enlighten these boys to become heroes. Each one of them has the heart for battle; we must remind them of the war they are currently involved in. One of the chief deceits that Lucifer has used on our militants is to convince them that the conflict does not exist; we cannot let this happen. If these boys do not grow to become warriors and men of honor, we will lose them. The Commander created them to fight, so fight they will!"

As Zachareal kept watch over the lad, named by his parents Michael (after the great Archangel that Zachareal had only had the opportunity to go into battle with once), he observed that Michael's parents were adherents of the Pillar of Truth (the Catholic Church). Proud of his young squire, Zachareal was there the day he was baptized. As the priest poured the water over the young militant's head Zachareal saw the spiritual chainmail that wrapped around the boy, almost as if a blanket of dense light swaddled him; each chain threaded its way in and out until the entire coat covered the boy from head to toe. Link by link, the spiritual body armor intertwined itself into the soul of the child; there was no longer a child and the chainmail; they were now one and the same. Kneeling around Michael were four choirs of angels singing Gloria in Excelsis Deo, the order of Cherubim surrounding the priest and child. Zachareal drew his sword, knelt down in front of his squire and lifted his sword with both hands as if offering it to Michael and bowed his head in reverence. In Zachareal's nephesh, better known to mortal men as his heart, he knew that the adventure ahead was to be a monumental one.

The day of Michael's initiation into the order of militants was the first time that Zachareal met Miknesha, a fallen angel from the 3rd hall of Hell. Zachareal had met many demons of the order of Mortium similar to Miknesha. They appeared to be a mirror image of Sentinels, but distorted and darkened somehow. Zachareal was a massive being, muscles bulging underneath his armor. His auburn hair flowed to his shoulders, and his piercing green eyes shone like the stars. His hands were as massive as frying pans, calloused yet soft at the same time. Miknesha, by contrast, was a sad and disjointed creature, appearing to be a starved, disheveled little demon whose head was covered with gristly strands of burnt thread. His intestinal organs could be seen moving underneath his sore-covered skin. While Sentinels held swords of gold and light, many of the Mortium kept swords of scuffed onyx, as black and misshapen as the Pillar of Deception. Sentinels donned helmets and breastplates with beatific designs inscribed on them, each and every piece of armor engrained with a small amount of blood from the Son of The Commander, not only helping with the bonding process but also intertwining the Divine Power of Protection. Mortium did not wear helmets or much armor; the fire from below had changed their once beautiful skin into a crust of sorts, hardened and begrimed from the hatred that rules the underworld of Lucifer. There is no need for armor where callousness reigns.

Zachareal knew that Miknesha was up to no good, and probably after his young squire. "I presume you have a reason for rising from the sepulcher of inferno?" Zachareal enquired.

Each word as wretched as the next, Miknesha answered, "Out of my way, Sentinel of the Enemy, I have a job to do and you will not stop me. I will never understand why you altruists consistently care for the waste! They mean nothing and my master gives them what they deserve." Miknesha's eyes, glowing like coals, burned brighter as he spoke hatefully of mortals. Curious to see what Miknesha planned to do, Zachareal tolerated his presence. Instead of going after Michael, Miknesha slithered over to Michael's father and rather than enticing him to gaze at the scantily clad woman in the front row, he decided to whisper in his ear a thought of how ridiculously archaic these rituals were. Michael's father had not been raised in a Catholic household; Michael's Grandfather's faith was nothing too serious, but his Grandmother took her Baptist faith very seriously. Miknesha knew this and used it to his advantage. "As my ole' guru used to say, 'if you want to destroy the scum, invite the males into spiritual spinelessness...'" Miknesha uttered to Zachareal, with a sly and grimacing smirk on his devilish face.

Zachareal unsheathed his sword, with light bright as the sun, pointed it at Miknesha and warned him, "If I ever see you skulking around my squire again, I'll beat you mercilessly and send you back to the maggot hole from whence you came! Be gone, Mortium!" With that, Miknesha disappeared, knowing that he had no chance against a Sentinel.

PHASE 2: WARRIOR AT HEART
"To be prepared for war is one of the most effectual means of preserving peace." ~ *General George Washington*

Michael grew up as many of the young militants did. One of Zachareal's fondest memories occurred during Michael's first phase of militancy. Michael was a curious and adventuresome little bloke, constantly testing his abilities by climbing higher and eating anything he could get his grasp on. One day Michael decided to wiggle his way out into the backyard where he loved to watch the birds. He walked around picking up as many sticks as he could and began to construct something. Zachareal was thoroughly fascinated with Michael's project. *What is he building?* Zachareal pondered.

As the sticks began to build up he noticed it appeared to be a stronghold of some kind. Without warning Michael jumped out of the sticks with the largest one in his hand swinging ferociously at an imagined enemy. "Back, you monster!" Michael cried, parrying left and right with the look of a livid combatant on his face. As he fought off his imaginary adversary, Zachareal had to shield his eyes due to the intensity of the light with which the spiritual chainmail given at his baptism glowed. The more passionate the young squire grew the brighter and thicker the light illumined.

The words of Raphael resounded in Zachareal's ears, they were created to fight! Until that moment, Zachareal had not fully understood what Raphael meant. The only other place he had seen that magnitude of illumination was at the bridal feast of the Lamb at the foot of the throne of The Commander. Michael was a good kid growing up. His heart was led by the ideas of honor and courage at a very young age. Zachareal did all he could with his angelic influence and power to keep those notions in Michael's head so that they were engrained into the fibers of his being.

Michael attended St. Catherine's Elementary School only a few miles away from his house. An elderly priest by the name of Patrick O'Connor was the religion teacher there. He was a man of the Baltimore Catechism and tried to use it in his classes as much as the other teachers would allow. His fellow instructors believed Fr. O'Connor was out of touch with the rest of the educational world. Comments such as not in touch with his feminine side and holds onto outdated philosophies and theology, and the worst of them all, too manly, regularly appeared on the desks of the Principal and the Superintendent. Zachareal, on the other hand, connected with this priest's Sentinel, Harachel, and made sure that this man was an integral part of Michael's upbringing. When going through the classes for First Communion, Zachareal knew that this Fr. O'Connor's influence would be fundamental to Michael's appreciation of the gift he was to receive. Zachareal recollected that during his own training the Cherubim taught him that the sacraments of Reconciliation and the Most Holy Eucharist were essential to the salvation of mortal men. They taught that without these two rites no man on earth could withstand the temptations of Lucifer. Zachareal influenced his young squire to listen with all his mind, heart and strength to the instruction of Fr. O'Connor.

During one of the classes Fr. O'Connor explained what would happen to the communicant's souls after receiving forgiveness in Confession and the body, blood, soul and divinity of Our Lord in Holy Communion.

"Your souls will be wiped clean of any hurtful or wrong actions that you have taken in the past. It is similar to seeing a shield after battle. Covered in blood, or worse, the shield loses its entire splendor from the previous battle. Jesus knows that our shields will eventually have blood upon them as none of us are perfect, but a good soldier cannot fight with a dirty shield. His shield must radiate the beauty and magnificence of that which he fights for. You all fight for the cause of Christ; a noble and worthy battle is before you. Reconciliation is the rite by which you return your shields to their proper elegance. The Most Holy Sacrament of the altar, The Eucharist, is the required weapon given His soldiers to keep that shield clean. As the Spartans used to say, 'come back with your shield or on it'." Michael's heart leaped in his chest; he couldn't wait until he was trained enough to receive his Lord.

A few months passed with the continuance of Sunday school and the teachings on the sacraments ahead until the day of the class's First Reconciliation. Michael was very nervous, but inside he was honored and content that he was going to Fr. O'Connor for confession. St. Catherine's had the traditional confessionals, made of dark oak with detailed edges and the priest in the middle of two kneelers. As Michael knelt down, Zachareal began to pray to the Omnipotent Fire of The Commander, the Third Person of the Holy Trinity. "Master, most holy animus of The Commander, look down upon my young squire today. Just as you were with Moses in the mountain, be with Michael. Enlighten his heart, strengthen his soul, and help him make a good first confession. Through our Queen Lady I pray. Amen."

Fr. O'Connor slipped back the screen and started, "In the name of the Father, and of the Son, and of the Holy Spirit." "Father, this is my first confession." As Michael began, Zachareal noted two Exousies, or Authority angels, came down upon young

Michael, with their eyes closed and hands folded; they were whispering prayers to the Omnipotent Fire. With each sin confessed to the priest, a large chalice of silver ornamented with enflamed gems came down from above towards the two Exousies angels. As the priest raised his right arm in absolution the angels tipped the goblet and crimson red blood as thick as molten rock ran out and poured over the soul of Michael, and each dark spot on the baptismal chainmail singed off and vanished. Michael ended his session the same way it began, in the name of the Holy Trinity. After he was done with his penance in front of the Blessed Sacrament he went to his mother and said, "I feel weightless, Mother! I can't wait to receive Communion!" Michael, knowing he had never seen his father go, couldn't wait to go home and tell him about the experience of confession.

After Michael's confession, Zachareal praised The Commander for His mercy and forgiveness. When he opened his eyes, he saw Miknesha leaning against the back door of the church with his arms folded across his chest and his bat-like wings shaking behind him. Miknesha's face was squelched with anger and his mouth was drooling out smoke. Staring at Zachareal with a look of doom on his face he telepathically communicated with him, growling out, "This time I will not lose... these half-breeds can dream all they want. Thinking that a Savior will keep them from the sulfuric underworld of screams and gnashing of teeth! Ha! They are more oblivious to the power below than you are, my nemesis! Yes; let them confess to the collared ape, let them believe that the fun they are having is wrong. I have a blueprint for this one that not even the mighty Zachareal, yes I know who you are, can stop. Once my chains are draped around this one I will rip him apart!" Zachareal glared at the Mortium with indignation, and with his right hand beat the Sentinel breastplate three times. War was about to ensue. Smoke arose where Miknesha had been standing and crept through the slit in between the double doors at the back of the church; Miknesha had vanished.

Michael arrived home that evening and went straight to the living room. Giddy with excitement, he ran up to his father to tell him about his recent experience. His father was on the couch watching the NBA playoff game between the L.A. Lakers and the Oklahoma City Thunder. Paperwork was sprawled out on the coffee table brought home from his job as a C.P.A. at Edmonds and Sons, one of the most respected law offices in their hometown. A full Miller Lite, accompanied by several other empty bottles, sat near the paper work.

"Dad, guess what!?!"

"What's up, Michael?" his father replied.

"Fr. O'Connor forgave me my sins today! I told mom that I feel light as a feather! My penance was only two Hail Mary's so I must not have hurt Jesus too bad!"

"Good son, now please go to your room and change out of your church clothes while I talk to your mother." Michael raced off to his room, too excited to sit still anyway.

"So you brought Michael to Fr. O'Connor?" Michael's father asked his wife.

"I did. I know you disagree with some of the homilies that Father has said in the past, but he is a good man and our Michael really looks up to him."

"I thought I told you that antiquated ole' kook should have retired years ago. Don't you remember what he told us when we got married? 'I know many of your generation are using birth control but I can tell you the Church will never allow it.' Then he pulled me aside and said that he was counting on me to look out for your womb! He thinks that collar allows him to say whatever he wants!"

"I know, babe, but I have come to realize that the Church knows what it's talking about, plus, you know I always wanted another child. I love Michael more than life itself, but I feel in my heart that he needs a sibling."

"Great, so now he has my wife pitted against me. Well, I can tell you right now, don't you dare stop taking those pills. What are we, animals?" With that, Michael's mother left the kitchen and went to the master bedroom disappointed in her husband but still feeling that she made the right decision to bring her son to Fr. O'Connor. Michael's father went back to the couch took a swig of his beer and couldn't believe that Oklahoma City was up by 10 over his beloved Lakers.

Blood of God

"As this sublime Sacrament towers above the others in dignity and efficacy, it is the most terrible of all weapons to the infernal powers." – Lorenzo Scupoli, The Spiritual Combat

The next day Michael's father woke Michael out of a deep, peaceful sleep. He whispered to his son, "Michael, we have to go visit Grandpa today. Get dressed; we'll be leaving in about 30 minutes. I've got breakfast on the table." Michael and his father ate breakfast together and then got in the 2012 Mercedes-Benz to head to Grandpa Joe's house. Michael's mother rarely went to Grandpa Joe's; when Michael's mother and father were married Grandpa Joe was disappointed to see his son convert from his Baptist background, not from the pride of his Baptist faith but stemming more from anti-Catholicism. "Those papists are nothing but trouble, son; you call yourself an American, yet you are bowing to a goof in a pointy hat!" Michael's father didn't care much about being a Baptist, so when he converted at his wedding it didn't mean much to him, but Grandpa Joe never let the feeling of disappointment leave him.

When Michael and his father arrived at Grandpa Joe's house he was where they expected him to be, sitting on his favorite lawn chair on his front porch, usually playing chess by himself; but this time he was just enjoying the beautiful day with a nice glass of scotch. Grandpa Joe was a Vietnam veteran and a tough old bloke to boot. He bottled up much resentment towards anyone besides what he most notably called a "WASP" (White Anglo-Saxon Protestant). He believed it was the WASP's that made America great and everyone else was out to get what they had.

"Hey Grandpa Joe!" exclaimed Michael.

"How's my Mikey doing?" replied Grandpa Joe.

Michael nearly shouted, "Wonderful Grandpa, I couldn't wait to tell about what happened at St. Catherine's!"

At that moment Michael's father made a sound as if he was clearing his throat to get Michael to stop talking. Grandpa Joe looked at his son and rolled his eyes in frustration, then walked into the front room of his house and snatched three fishing rods and a tackle box. He handed Michael his rod and they began walking towards the creek. Once a month the three generations would enjoy some time together fishing in the creek near the back of Grandpa Joe's property. This was a relished time for young Michael; he loved his Grandpa very much and knew that he loved him back. The war stories Grandpa would share with him sparked Michael's attention like nothing else could. On this day, however, Grandpa Joe did not want to discuss his past; he wanted to discuss Michael's future. Michael and his Grandfather walked together to the other side of the creek while Michael's father stayed near the tackle box.

Zachareal noticed from a distance Miknesha grinning from horn to horn with a dastardly look on his face, holding a long, black, twisted chain in his hand. Zachareal flew across the lake directly towards Miknesha. As Zachareal arrived, Miknesha seemed to stand his ground ready for a fight; Zachareal swooped in, grabbed Miknesha's throat and slammed him against a tree behind him. Zachareal's face, writhing in anger, yelled out, "What do you think you are doing here, you abominable creature of death?"

With smoke oozing from his nostrils and black vile draining from his mouth, Miknesha replied, "My job".

Zachareal looked behind the tree to see the other end of the chain Miknesha was holding, and saw a poor Sentinel was wrapped up inside the black mess. Zachareal smashed Miknesha's head into the tree, glared with his emerald green eyes and solemnly said, "Leave or I'll rip your head clean off." Miknesha, once again, vanished. As Zachareal moved over to the tied up Sentinel, he noticed that his wings were missing many feathers and that the light emanating from his weapon was dull. The Sentinel's ruffled body was war-torn from years of harsh battles with the Mortium. Though angels receive their powers from the Commander, the battle at hand is very real and wounds can be sustained when the militant does not cooperate with Divine Grace. Zachareal asked him, "What has happened here?"

The disheveled angel, breathing deeply stated, "Fellow Warrior of The Commander, I am the Sentinel of the Grandfather to your squire. Joseph has all but forgotten his faith and no longer fights for anything good or beautiful. Due to his lack of honor and courage my poor self has been ruffled. I fear I am losing the soul I am meant to protect." As the pitiable spirit spoke, Zachareal heard Michael speaking with his Grandfather.

"Mikey, I need to talk to you about this St. Catherine's." extorted Grandpa Joe.

With a big smile on his face, Michael replied, "I would love to!"

"Mikey, there comes a time in every man's life when he must decide whether he will be a king or a pawn." (Grandpa Joe was a big fan of Napoleon Bonaparte.) "Whether or not he will allow his own reason and conscience to rule his life or if he will allow someone else to tell him what to believe. Now, you know that I am not a Catholic like your parents. I don't believe in all of the superstition and nonsense of old women."

"But, Grandpa. It's not nonsense. Fr. O'Connor has explained everything to me. It's about being a fighter, about having a cause worth dying for." countered Michael.

"Well, that's all good and well, son, but that ole' potato-eatin' priest of yours has been fed the lies for many years and now he believes it." Grandpa Joe said with certainty. "I feel obligated to tell you that he doesn't know what's good for you. You'll figure it out when you get older."

"Okay, Grandpa, but the feelings I felt after confession yesterday did not feel like nonsense to me." Michael answered.

The next day Michael woke up early to get his suit and tie on. He ran downstairs for breakfast, ate his bacon and eggs and rushed out to the car ready to go to St. Catherine's to receive the armament that Father O'Connor had spoken of. In his mind he wanted to keep his shield as clean as a whistle, but he couldn't help recalling what Grandpa Joe told him at the creek. On the way to Mass, Michael racked his brain to figure out exactly what he believed. "Is the fight Fr. O'Connor was talking about real? Or is Grandpa right?" He wanted to believe in the ideals of his Faith, but he couldn't help thinking that what Grandpa said might be true. When Michael arrived at St. Catherine's he decided he would wait until he received communion to make a final decision on what exactly he believed. He was very excited to see that it was Fr. O'Connor who would be celebrating Mass.

During the homily Fr. O'Connor explained exactly what was going to happen to the communicants. He said that these young boys and girls were about to take the next step in their relationship with Christ, and that this gift given by the Savior would strengthen them enough to face the ominous world they were venturing into. Michael was glued to Fr. O'Connor as he spoke. Father would glance at Michael during his discourse and Michael felt as though he was peering into his very heart. Fr. O'Connor finished by stating that "…this Bread from Heaven is what Our Lord allows us to receive in order to become homesick, because we are all Kings in exile."

While the representatives of the faithful brought forth the gifts, Zachareal noticed that angels, many of whom he remembered from his days of training, descended upon the priest as he prepared for the Holy Sacrifice. Each angel gave the impression that they were organizing the ranks for something big to happen. As the angels fell in line, Zachareal detected Miknesha, his sworn enemy, once again standing menacingly at the back of the church. Knowing that what was about to happen was far too important to be distracted from, Zachareal ignored the demon, and focused on the ritual at hand. As the priest raised the consecrated host, three peals of bells rang out and Zachareal heard a blood-curdling scream from the back of the church. Looking back he saw that Miknesha had left, and when he gazed back at the host it had become something different entirely. The Host had changed into a beating heart surrounded by a crown of thorns, dripping blood onto the other hosts, changing them into tiny pieces of flesh, each of them radiating a light. The altered pieces within the bowl pulsated, as if breathing, beating to the same rhythm as the Host held up by the priest.

Then the priest raised the chalice; again three bells rang out. Zachareal witnessed bright red drops flowing from the crucifix hanging above the altar, red as rubies, each bead of blood as bright as the stars in the heavens. The dripping sap drenched the communicants as they received what originally was wine yet now is the blood of Agnus Dei. The rest of the angels began a melodic hymn, 'Verus Amori Nunquam Mori'. Zachareal fell to his face and prostrated himself before the occurring miracle. When it was Michael's turn to receive the Blessed Sacrament, Zachareal went with him praying for his young militant. Looking at Fr. O'Connor, Zachareal realized that The Son of The Commander had taken the place of the priest, almost as if it were an optical illusion. Zachareal could still see the priest, but The Son, had draped himself over him as though a translucent slip had wrapped itself around the mortal.

As each communicant approached the altar of sacrifice, The Son's face brightened with affection. With the angels singing and praising the name of love, it was quite unanticipated to see The Son occasionally disheartened, which only occurred when some of the men would arrive to receive, dressed as if they were about to go to a sporting event or perhaps the beach, disinterestedly taking the gift with the look of entitlement. But Zachareal detected that He never lost heart or mercy for His Father's creation. His heart beat louder and with more force for the men he pitied. As Michael knelt after his reception, his earnest prayer consisted of asking for a sign or a feeling of fulfillment to confirm or deny his questions. Zachareal knew that the Gift was not about feelings or spiritual highs, but rather duty and honor; he knew those feelings wouldn't come unless The Commander willed it. He knew that a true soldier does not require mood changes and that asking for them was a sign of weakness. Zachareal's nephesh went out to his young militant, but despite his prayers, Michael's doubt crept in. Michael's faith was never the same.

PHASE 3: THE DRUMS OF BATTLE
"A man cannot become a hero until he can see the root of his own downfall." ~ Aristotle

Years passed and Michael continued to grow physically; spiritually, his growth had been stifled since the day of his conversation with Grandpa Joe. Regardless of the unfortunate circumstances Zachareal continued his mission with heart and pride in Michael. Three years after Michael's first communion Zachareal had yet another confrontation with Miknesha. Michael went to meet his cousin Jason, who was a decent militant, but far from a fighter. The Mortium demon assigned to Jason had thoroughly addicted him to the deadly disease of pornography. Pornography was the downfall of many good men, its effect on the spiritual chainmail of militants poisonous. More than just staining and burning it, it creates a weak link, thus weakening the entire defense in line with the old saying, A chain is only as good as its weakest link.

When Michael went to meet his cousin, Jason invited him into his room to see something on the computer. Michael was exceedingly ashamed by what he saw, "Jason, I shouldn't be watching this and neither should you!" Michael ripped the cord out of the wall and ran outside to think about what had just happened. Miknesha laughed demonically, pointed at Zachareal from a distance and teasingly said, "The seed is planted Zachareal, the battle begins! After you get them once, it is a greasy slope from here. Soon, Zachareal, very soon, I will have this monkey eating out of the dumpster and begging for more. As I told you before, invite these so-called men into a door of weakness and you won't even have to kick them through. Warriors, heh! Look how feeble they become with one tiny suggestion!"

Zachareal wept, knowing that after seeing such filth his poor militant's mind would never be the same. Zachareal knew that with the grace of the Omnipotent Fire, the regular use of confession and devotion to the Queen Mother, this enticement could be overcome. However, he also knew that Michael was not a strong enough fighter to resist the continual temptation thrown in the face of so many militants. He raised his massive arms to the heavens and yelled, "Master! Commander! Take pity on my Michael!" Michael never told anyone what had happened; he didn't want his older cousin to get in trouble. He buried the experience deep within himself and justified it by saying that he was not at fault, thus there was no need to say anything in confession.

Years went by, during which Michael begged his father to let him have his own computer for his room. Well off and secure financially, Michael's father bought him one the next day, even though Michael's mother disagreed with the purchase, one of the many arguments the two of them were having during this time in their lives. Initially Michael wanted the computer for his school assignments and games to play. But Miknesha had a nasty tendency to roam around waiting for Michael to turn on the computer. Wrapping his chains around the device Miknesha took control of everything that happened on it. Zachareal was not powerless against a scheme like this, but it was Michael's free will that would decide the use of the computer. After a month of owning the device Michael was spending more time in front of it than any other hobby. He drifted away from his friends and lost the desire to pray. Hours were spent in an alternate-reality video game, finished by clicking on the advertisement for Girls Gone Wild. During these long periods of time spent in front of the computer, Miknesha would drape Michael's soul in a dark shadow and wallop it with the bullwhip of terror.

Before he knew it, Michael was spending all of his allowance on the latest game systems and multiplied the purchases with mounds and mounds of games to go with them. His favorite game was Sin City, in which the player worked for the mob in Las Vegas. The game began with the player proving himself to the "Outfit" by murdering someone who owed him money and starting up a prostitution ring. The feelings generated from playing these games reminded him of his childhood, dreaming of fighting for a cause and a brotherhood, repetitively telling himself, "At least the rush I feel with these games is closer to reality than a child's imagination."

Michael stopped going to church with his mother, thinking that Grandpa Joe had it right all along; besides, his father never went, so why should he? At sixteen he began drinking with his friends from school. Michael's father decided to pull him out of St. Catherine's hoping that public school would offer more opportunity for sports. Nightly parties and "hooking-up" became a frequent ritual for Michael. Zachareal, weakened from the years of Michael's sins, cried daily for his young squire. "What happened to the warrior that I knew? In such a short time he has become a coward and a weakling!" Miknesha'a power grew daily while Zachareal's wings shed and lost their once radiant color. At a loss, Zachareal decided to ask for advice from one of his old trainers. He confided in Virtureal, the angel of The Commander sent to Joseph, Virgin Husband of the Queen Mother, before the Savior was born. If any angel knew how to call men to battle, it was him.

"Sir, my militant has left The Pillar of Truth and I fear that he is travelling a road that I cannot follow." Zachareal pleaded.

"Sentinel, it saddens me to see the state of men in the physical realm. I must advise you what The Commander advised me when Joseph thought of leaving Mary, 'Call him to war, Virtureal!' he said, and then imparted me with the message of hope that I then conveyed to the carpenter." Virtureal responded.

Zachareal, slightly confused, questioned, "Sire, are you suggesting what I think you are?"

Virtureal with all the calmness of the choir of Archangels nodded his head in approval. In order to give Zachareal some hope, Virtureal ended their conversation telling him, "Mortal men must know of the perpetual conflict they are involved in. The Commander allowed spiritual combat so that the souls of men would have fulfillment. They desire something to die for, or else they don't feel they deserve to live. Lucifer knows this, and has chosen to weaken their wills to fight! After I sent a small inspiration of battle to the ever powerful warrior Joseph, my knight for many years, he was able to fight and die with his shield. He has called men to war and now it is time for you to inspire your militant! Do what is necessary to save his soul!" Zachreal then understood what must be done.

PHASE 4: WRIT OF RESOLUTION

"Of men who have a sense of honor, more come through alive than are slain, but from those who flee comes neither glory nor any help." ~ Homer, The Iliad

Michael grew into a very handsome man. A member of Lambda Pi, he graduated with a bachelor's in computer engineering, hoping to design video games for one of the larger companies in the U.S. Most of his college career was spent drinking and filled with one-night stands with women, most of whose names he couldn't remember the next day. After college, his parents divorced and his mother moved back home to live with her parents until she could find a suitable home. Michael gave the impression that he was indifferent to his parents' split, but Zachareal could see what had occurred within his soul. When Michael received the news from his mother, Zachareal saw the only weapon left in Michael's spiritual arsenal, his foot guards, fall off and get left behind.

After witnessing the fragmented relationship of his own parents Michael never desired to have a long-standing relationship with a woman, until at age 32, he met Rachel. Rachel was from a wealthy family and very well known for her beauty. After three months of dating, Rachel and Michael moved in together. Michael never promised a ring or a future of any kind, but Rachel still kept the hope of marriage and possibly a family within the next couple of years. Time continued but Michael seemed to stand still. Rachel quickly began to complain about the amount of time that he spent playing Madden Football or World of Warcraft. After a year of living together, Rachel was tired of acting more as a mother figure than as a girlfriend. Several times she caught him watching pornography and his only excuse was that "it's a guy thing, you wouldn't understand!"

When Zachareal and Miknesha would interact, each time Miknesha had a new ornament or weapon of some kind, rewards for sins committed by his client. By now Zachareal had been weakened to the point that his once booming voice now sounded like that of a lifelong smoker. Zachareal's threats meant very little to Miknesha now. Before Rachel decided to move out, Miknesha told Zachareal, "Defeated enemy, the maggot you tried to save has now lived down to my standards for many years. You might as well hang up that poor excuse of a sword you hold. His soul is as good as mine! Since you are so deteriorated and powerless now, I might as well tell you what Michael's future holds. The girl he now takes advantage of has just found out that she is with child; it makes me gag just thinking about it! I have no need to worry though, my good friends at the women's clinic will help her, and Michael will walk her right through the front door! Can you believe they call it a clinic? We have done well with the vocabulary, haven't we? Well, Zachareal,", Miknesha now had the gall to get close to his enemy, rubbing his twisted little fingers across the Sentinel breastplate, smiling and giggling, "I hope I don't need to tell you that the next time I see you, Michael will seal the deal…"

The only thoughts that came to Zachareal's mind were those of Virtureal. He recalled the story of St. Joseph and his comprehensive role in the salvation of men. The Commander chose a man to raise His own son, and of it weren't for Virtureal, would the Savior have had what he needed to become the man he was destined to be? Just the thought of Michael's soul drifting through the gates of Hell made Zachareal writhe in anger. He knelt down and asked The Omnipotent Fire for one last opportunity to take a stand against Miknesha and the struggles of this world. "Most Holy Master, give me the strength needed to help Michael one last time. Allow me to give the last bit of blood, sweat, and tears that I have to save his soul. In the name of Our Queen Mother, I pray." Suddenly Zachareal felt a burning in his armor, his atrophied muscles filled out once again and his sword shone brighter than it ever had before. More invigorated than the day of Michael's initiation into the order of militants, Zachareal rose from his knees, unsheathed his sword and slammed his fist against his breastplate three times, hankering once again for combat.

Zachareal found Miknesha outside of a confession booth just waiting for people to exit and to remind them of their sins and, with a little luck, to get them to doubt their forgiveness. From the corner of his eye Miknesha noticed Zachareal, but did not recognize him at first. As soon as they made eye contact Zachareal swooped over and thrashed Miknesha across the church. He flew over to him, grabbed his worn leather wings and threw him outside. Miknesha, caught completely off guard, was too slow to react. By the time he rose to his hooves Zachareal was already on top of him, beating him with his shield. Finally, the enraged angel of God took out his sword, lifted Miknesha by his grisly horns, and beheaded him. Being that Mortium are immortal, Miknesha's shadow squirmed in pain for a moment then sunk to the 3rd hall of Hell from whence he originated. Zachareal's next act was to pursue Michael and follow in Virtureal's footsteps.

Zachareal found Michael at his home, sitting in front of his newly acquired seventy-two-inch flat screen television. Michael was playing a military first-man shooter game with music blaring in the background. Through his headset he was speaking to someone across the world playing the same game. Zachareal suddenly had a flashback, thinking of all the beautiful memories he had with Michael: the time he fell out of the rickety tree house Michael built and Zachareal caught him just before he hit the ground so that no bones were broken; his time with Michael during Fr. O'Connor's religion classes, watching Michael's soul glow with pride; seeing Michael's eyes the first time they opened radiating the light of his Creator. In a flash Zachareal also remembered the first time he met Miknesha; swiftly Zachareal's blood began to boil. Angels cannot feel hate, but a righteous anger is one of their gifts. Roused to zeal by that gift, Zachareal prayed to the Savior and thought about the best possible plan of action.

Just as Michael shot one of the imaginary enemies in his game, the electricity went out. In the blink of an eye a bright light appeared in front of him and a booming voice belted out, "Michael! Michael! Do not be afraid!" Michael crawled up the back of his couch, scared to death of the vision before him.

"What are you?" Michael screamed.

"I have been with you since the beginning, my young militant. I am the Sentinel angel sworn to protect you. Zachareal is my name, Guardian of The Commander and fourth Sargent of the order of Warrior Angels," Zachareal responded.

Michael, still shielding his eyes from the light, asked, "What do you want from me?"

"I only want to help you. You were born for a very specific purpose; saving souls and protecting women is why you were born, Michael. All this time I have been watching you, holding you close to my heart. I've seen your struggles, I know your temptations and failures, but I also see the heart of a lion within you! Don't you remember the times we had in the back yard, building forts and fighting monsters? What has happened, Michael? Where is the fighter that I know you are? Your Lord and Savior has given you everything that is necessary to fight and die with honor and purpose. Somewhere along the way you gave up! You decided that you'd rather be a coward and claim happiness in this world rather than live for the noble ideals of the next! Life is not one big party, Michael. A man must do what is necessary to be a hero!" Michael could see the veins popping out of the neck and biceps of Zachareal as he spoke. Zachareal continued, "You think that you have no purpose in life; you've allowed others to swindle you into a life of spinelessness. I am here to tell you that this is not LIFE! You are in the midst of a war, Michael; you are on the front lines! Principalities and powers, the rulers of the world of darkness, are out to slay and murder you and your kin. They want to feast on the flesh of your loved ones, and what are you doing about it? Nothing! You sit here in an alternate reality and use women for your own heartless pleasure. You call yourself a man, yet I see no gall, no wit, no integrity. I want to call you back, Michael; the battle is not over, you can still fight, 'you must fight to conquer your enemy and anyone who tries to ruin you. Be courageous. Do not be afraid or cowardly. Christ your Captain is here with all the power of Heaven to protect you from the enemy, and to see that they never conquer you, either by brute power, or by trickery. Hold your ground! Do violence to yourself, no matter how painful it is. Call out for the help of Jesus and Mary and all the Saints. If you do this, you will be victorious.'* I will always be with you, Michael, from the depths to the heights. It will be an honor to fight by your side; stand up and be the man God created you to be!"

After that Zachareal knelt down, bowed his head, beat his Sentinel breastplate three times, looked up at Michael and peered into his eyes with the look of an aching desire for Truth. Zachareal vanished; the electricity came back on along with the noise of the music and game. Michael turned everything off and began to sob, he then fell to his knees and prayed.

* Short quote taken from Lorenzo Scupoli's *The Spiritual Combat*

Jared Zimmerer - a husband and father of four, Jared is the founder of Strength for the Kingdom, a Texas-based ministry promoting men's growth in virtue, knowledge of the Catholic faith, and the understanding of authentic masculinity through physical endeavors. He is the author of *The Ten Commandments of Lifting Weights* and a frequent contributor to Fr. Robert Barron's *Word on Fire* blog. He is the Director of Adult Formation and Family Life Ministry at St. Francis of Assisi in Grapevine, Texas.

Dave DiNuzzo Sr. – a Catholic husband and father of four, Dave is the founder of TrueManhood Men's Ministry, a ministry calling men to fight cultural manliness© and live virtue. This speaker, author, blogger, retreat master, and evangelist, has served as a FOCUS Missionary, Director of Campus Ministry at the Air Force Academy, Director of Programming for a national men's ministry, and a Diocesan Director of Young Adult & Campus Ministry.

Douglas Bushman - Pope Saint John Paul II Chair for the New Evangelization at The Augustine Institute, this frequent guest of Catholic radio and television, and author of *In His Image: A Program of Renewal through Education*, is past Director of both the Institute for Religious and Pastoral Studies (University of Dallas), and Institute for Pastoral Theology (Ave Maria University)

Gerard-Marie Anthony - a professor at Christ the Teacher College, Gerard-Marie is the author of *Who Am I? A Theology of the Body in Prayer*, *The Four Keys to Sanctity*, and *Why Do Catholics Worship Mary?*

Jim Burnham - an apologist with Catholic Answers, Jim is the director of San Juan Catholic Seminars, a lay organization devoted to explaining and defending the Catholic Faith. He is

Deacon Harold Burke-Sivers - President and CEO of Servant Enterprises, Inc., a non-profit organization that also hosts an international institute for Catholic male spirituality, coordinates dynamic speaking tours and life-changing retreats, and develops products and services that support family life. He has hosted a number of EWTN television series, including *Behold the Man: Spirituality for Men* and *Authentically Free At Last*.

Fr. Steve Grunow - priest of the Archdiocese of Chicago and CEO of Word on Fire Catholic Ministries. He served as theological consultant and spiritual advisor to Fr. Robert Barron's monumental *Catholicism* series.

Jesse Romero - founder of On Fire Evangelization, Jesse is a bilingual, Catholic lay evangelist and a much sought after speaker. He co-hosts Ave Maria Radio Network's *The Terry and Jesse Show*, and has contributed to countless periodicals, radio and television programs, as well as the books *Welcome Home: Fallen Away Catholics Who Came Back* and *Freedom: 12 Lives Transformed by the Theology of the Body*.

Kevin Vost, Psy.D. - best-selling author and frequent guest of Catholic television and radio, this psychologist / college professor / Mensa member / body builder is the co-author *Christian Fatherhood* and co-hosted the popular EWTN series, *The Carpenter's Shop.*

Kevin Lowry - with over over twenty years in secular financial and executive management roles, this author of *Faith At Work: Finding Purpose Beyond the Paycheck* currently serves as Chief Operating Officer for Marcus Grodi's Coming Home Network International. His conversion was featured in Patrick Madrid's *Surprised By Truth 2: 15 Men and Women Give the Biblical and Historical Reasons For Becoming Catholic.*

Shane Kapler - this regular guest of Catholic radio was a long-time member of the Archdiocese of St. Louis' Retreat, Evangelization, and Prayer (REAP) Team. He is author of the books *Through, With, and In Him: The Prayer Life of Jesus and How to Make It Our Own, The God Who is Love: Explaining Christianity From Its Center,* and co-author of *Tending The Temple: 365 Days of Spiritual and Physical Devotions.*

well known for bringing the wisdom of St. Thomas Aquinas to the masses through titles such as *Unearthing Your Ten Talents, Fit For Eternal Life, Memorize the Faith!,* Catholic Answers' *Memorize the Reasons! The Catholic Art of Memory for Apologetics,* and *The One-Minute Aquinas.*

Marlon De La Torre - this former Diocesan Director of Religious Education for the Catholic Diocese of Memphis and Superintendent of Catholic Schools for the Catholic Diocese of Kansas City-St. Joseph, now serves as the Director of Catechist Formation and Children's Catechesis for the Catholic Diocese of Fort Worth. He is the author of *Screwtape Teaches the Faith: A Guide for Catechists,* a work paralleling C.S. Lewis' *Screwtape Letters* with the *Catechism of the Catholic Church.*

CPSIA information can be obtained at www.ICGtesting.com
Printed in the USA
LVOW01s0223100414

381089LV00021BA/382/P